Messiah

Messiah

Paul Barnett

Messiah

Jesus - the evidence of history

ivp

INTER-VARSITY PRESS
Norton Street, Nottingham NG7 3HR, England
Email: ivp@ivpbooks.com
Website: www.ivpbooks.com

First published 2009

British Library Cataloguing in Publication Data
A catalogue record for this book is available from the British Library.

ISBN: 978-1-84474-352-0

Set in Monotype Garamond 11/13pt
Typeset in Great Britain by Servis Filmsetting Ltd, Stockport, Cheshire
Printed and bound in Great Britain by Ashford Colour Press Ltd,
Gosport, Hampshire.

Inter-Varsity Press publishes Christian books that are true to the Bible and that
communicate the gospel, develop discipleship and strengthen the church for its
mission in the world.

Inter-Varsity Press is closely linked with the Universities and Colleges Christian
Fellowship, a student movement connecting Christian Unions in universities and
colleges throughout Great Britain, and a member movement of the International
Fellowship of Evangelical Students. Website: www.uccf.org.uk.

CONTENTS

PREFACE

Ten years ago I wrote *Jesus and the Rise of Early Christianity* (Downers Grove: IVP, 1999), a book whose title needs little explanation. My thesis was that Jesus' identity and achievements as the Christ (or Messiah) were the engine that accounted for the rise of Christianity and drove its earliest history. This present book is a kind of companion volume, which focuses more on Jesus the Messiah himself.

As in the earlier book, I have attempted to write more from a historical than a theological perspective. Soundly based evidence is the basis for historical writing and this applies as forcefully to Jesus of Nazareth as to Augustus, the emperor in whose times Jesus was born. Dogmatic statements can be made both for and against Jesus and Christian origins, but they are self-cancelling and are ultimately of little use. *Evidence* is everything.

Accordingly, I am excited when I locate multiple witnesses to various aspects of Jesus. These tell me I can regard this evidence with considerable confidence. For such critical areas as Jesus' mission and identity and his miracles and resurrection we do indeed have what is called *multiple attestation*, which I shall point out along the way.

In the spirit of self-disclosure, let me identify myself as a mainstream Christian believer. Inevitably, my faith perspective influences what I write. At the same time, however, I attempt to write with the objectivity of a historian.

1. GOD, THE MESSIAH AND HISTORY

Finding out about Jesus the Messiah is connected in the closest possible way with finding out about God. My purpose in writing is to demonstrate that finding out about Jesus is straightforward and within reach of all of us.

The Messiah and the invisible Creator

That God the Creator is invisible to the human eye is something we all accept. Yet the remarkable claim of the New Testament is that the unseen, intangible Creator has made himself known to the human senses of sight, hearing and touch, and that he has done so in Jesus the Messiah.

> No one has ever seen God; the only Son, who is at the Father's side, he has *made him known*. (John 1:18; my tr.)[1]

> In [Christ] the whole fullness of deity dwells *bodily*. (Col. 2:9)

These assertions are the more significant because the writers John and Paul were Jews for whom the idea of God coming in human form would have been blasphemous. The Second Commandment prohibited any visual portrayal of God, and the daily prayer (the Shema) taught that God is 'one', thereby excluding any idea that a man or angel could be regarded as a deity (Exod. 20:4; Deut. 6:4). Yet such was the impact of Jesus that these Jews were compelled to rethink their ideas about God radically. God had drawn near in the Messiah, Jesus.

The implication is breathtaking. The unseen God has shown himself and has done so not partially or as a passing glimpse, but fully and clearly. God has done this for a kindly purpose, to draw flawed and broken people like us into a loving and deeply personal relationship with him. God has made it possible for us to honour him by our dependence on him and in our joyous service of others. In other words, we humans find the otherwise mysterious meaning of life now revealed in knowing, loving and serving the One who has come to us.

God has revealed himself in this way in and through the adult man, the Messiah Jesus, at a particular time and place, that is, in Palestine in the era of the Roman emperor Tiberius. In other words, God has done this at a historical moment, as documented in the Gospels.

These Gospels have two unique but connected characteristics: they are historical biographies about Jesus back *then* (and would have been recognized as such at the time), but equally they are the word of God to us *now*. God meets us dynamically and spiritually as we read and hear the gospel, which is God's own and living word.

Atheists and history

Aggressive atheists who seek to disprove God make historical attacks on the New Testament as part of their strategy.[2] Their instincts are correct: destroy the historical credibility of the Gospels and you destroy the credibility of Jesus and thus destroy belief in God. Christopher Hitchens is clear: 'The case for biblical consistency or authenticity or "inspiration" has been in tatters for some time, and the rents and tears only become more obvious with better research, and thus no "revelation" can be derived from that quarter.'[3]

Hitchens is wide of the mark in asserting that 'the case for biblical consistency . . . has been in tatters', but is correct in seeing the importance of attacking the Bible as a way of discrediting belief in God.

This provokes the question 'How well do these prominent atheists know the Bible and its historical setting?' In fact, not well, despite their high qualifications in other disciplines.

Richard Dawkins, for example, refers to anecdotes about the boy Jesus in the *Gospel of Thomas* that he confuses with the *Infancy Story of Thomas*.[4] (The *Gospel of Thomas* contains no narrative storyline but is a collage of Jesus' words, transposed in mystical language.) Worse, Dawkins attributes the story of the Magi to the Gospel of Luke, when it actually appears in the Gospel of Matthew![5] Dawkins even goes so far as to question the existence of Jesus.[6] Here he depends on the opinions of Professor G. A. Wells, who is not a historian but a scholar in German studies. Reputable ancient historians irrespective of religious persuasion know that Jesus was a genuine figure of history. Again, Dawkins reveals his ignorance in ascribing a tribal harshness ('out-group hostility') to Jesus, as in Old Testament attitudes to non-Jews.[7] But Jesus' friendship with 'sinners' and social outcasts is one of the most secure historical details about him. Finally, Dawkins shows amazing ignorance in asserting the Gospels were as much works of fiction as Dan Brown's *Da Vinci Code*.[8] Biblical scholars of all stripes, to the contrary, have reached a consensus in viewing the Gospels as identifiable historical biographies.[9]

Another prominent atheist, Michel Onfray, thinks the hope of eternal life is based on the monotheistic faiths arising in the *desert*:

> I thought of the lands of Israel, Judaea and Samaria, of Jerusalem and Bethlehem, of Nazareth and the Sea of Galilee. Places where the sun bakes men's heads, desiccates their bodies, afflicts their souls with thirst. Places that generate a yearning for oases where water flows cool, clear and free, where the air is balmy and fragrant, where food and drink are abundant. The afterlife suddenly struck me as a counterworld invented

by men exhausted and parched by their ceaseless wanderings across the
dunes or up and down rocky trails baked to white heat.[10]

This is incorrect. Lakeside Galilee is admittedly hot in the summer
but in a subtropical, not desert, sense. It is a lush fertile area that
grows bananas, mangos and avocados in abundance.

More could be said. It is clear from these serious errors that
Hitchens, Dawkins and Onfray are not well informed about the
New Testament or its historical and geographical setting. Their
errors, however, serve to make us appreciate the true authenticity
of these texts in their contexts.

History, the Gospels and God

We cannot overstate the importance of the Gospels being historically true for our trust in God. George Ladd's words capture this
well.

> The uniqueness and the scandal of the Christian religion rests on the
> mediation of revelation through historical events. Christianity is not just
> a code for living or a philosophy of religion. It is rooted in the real
> events of history . . . is . . . bound up with the truth of certain historical
> facts. And if those facts should be disproved, Christianity would be false.
> This, however, is what makes Christianity unique because, unlike other
> world religions, modern man has means of actually verifying
> Christianity's truth by historical evidence.[11]

True as this is for Christianity in general, it is even more so for the
record in the Gospels about the Messiah Jesus, its founder.

Mere belief in the credibility of the Gospels, however, does not
in itself bring us into contact with God. This occurs as we hear
and personally engage with the Gospels' *message* of God's love
shown to us in Jesus. If, on the other hand, we have serious and
substantial doubts about the veracity of the texts, then it is difficult
for us to hear God speaking through them. The aggressive atheists
betray inferior knowledge of the New Testament but they are right
in seeing those texts as worthy targets of their attacks.

My argument in this book is that the information about Jesus the Messiah in the New Testament is soundly based according to high standards of historical analysis. We can be confident in believing Jesus' words as they appear in the Gospels and in the account of his death and resurrection for us. By doing so we are brought into the presence of God.

Multiple witnesses

Evidence is what I look for, if possible from more than one quarter. In that sense, a historian's craft is similar to the work of police investigators, lawyers and juries. One person's word is not as good as two. But the evidence of the second witness is of little use if she merely repeats what she has heard from the first. Two or more *independent* witnesses are better.

Historians of the distant past often have only one source of evidence for a person or event, but are grateful even for that. Only a fraction of written texts and inscriptions from antiquity have survived the wind and rain of the centuries. Lack of evidence probably means there is a gap in the overall mosaic, and it may be a vital gap, leaving us to guess who may have been there and what may have happened.

Inspired by the recent presence of Jesus of Nazareth, the New Testament is a slim collection of texts, composed of four historical works (Luke-Acts is one opus), twenty-one letters written to churches and individuals and one unusual letter-book, the Apocalypse. These texts from first to last were written in a narrow time band AD 48–95, but often depend on oral traditions created from and after the time of Jesus (AD 30–33). So the texts are remarkably close to Jesus, closer than for almost anyone from that era, and frequently represent merely the final written stage of a longer oral history.

John's Gospel is independent of the Gospels of Matthew, Mark and Luke. And underlying Matthew and Luke (in addition to Mark) are independent Gospel sources that have been called 'Q' (common to Matthew and Luke), 'L' (only in Luke) and 'M' (only in Matthew):

John
Mark
Q
L
M

Thus there are five primary and independent Gospel sources of information about Jesus. To these, however, we may add Matthew and Luke themselves, who contribute information to their respective Gospels beyond what they incorporate from their sources:[12]

Matthew
Luke

Five letter writers also contribute to the New Testament, independently of the Gospels' sources and of each other:[13]

Paul
Author of Hebrews
James
Peter
Jude

This is impressive. Together twelve independent sources of information about Christ are found in the body of texts we call the New Testament. This means that the historian who writes about Jesus and early Christianity has more (and early) source material than many famous figures of the era; for example, Tiberius, the emperor in whose time Jesus was crucified. Although these texts appear to be religious, they do not disregard history: in fact, quite the reverse.

Conclusion

The importance of historical evidence is inescapable, for without it the claims of the New Testament about Jesus would be merely mythological. Mythology is often 'interesting' or has 'helpful' insights into human nature. One thinks, for example, of Homer's story in the *Odyssey* (and from other sources) about the seductive music of the Sirens and the even more beautiful music of Orpheus delivering the Argonauts. The events portrayed did not actually happen but are interesting, meaningful and helpful, but had no concrete actuality.

The Gospels, however, present Jesus to us as one who is 'true' in every sense and therefore of absolute and eternal significance. The consequences of ignoring him are as dire as ignoring God the Father himself. Jesus uniquely connects us to the Father because God has first uniquely connected with us in Jesus the Messiah. Fundamental to that 'connecting' is the historical reality of Jesus' birth, life, teachings, death and resurrection. This is why sound evidence is vital.

2. KNOWING ABOUT JESUS

Since Jesus lived so long ago, we assume we know little about his life story. But this is untrue. In fact, we know more about him than about many famous people closer to our own times: William Shakespeare, for example. The quantity and quality of the documentary evidence is more important than whether someone lived a long time ago or recently.

We know about Jesus from the twenty-seven texts focused on him, written by nine different authors within a lifetime of his lifespan. Furthermore, although hostile to him, the non-Christian writers Josephus, Tacitus and Pliny corroborate the raw facts about Jesus and the character of early Christianity.

So what do we know about Jesus?

We can establish the perimeters of his lifespan: he was born in Bethlehem in circa 5 BC and was executed by the Romans at the instigation of the Jewish leaders in Jerusalem at the Passover of AD 30 or 33. His parents Joseph and Mary, both Jewish and from the tribe of Judah, lived in Nazareth, a tiny village in lower Galilee overlooking the Jezreel Valley, located midway between the Sea of Tiberias and the Mediterranean coast. He was the older brother of James, Joseph, Judas and Simon and of several (unnamed) sisters.

Jesus was an apprentice to his father, a craftsman working as a cutter of stone and timber. Joseph appears to have died when Jesus was a young adult, leaving him as the senior male in the family as he continued to follow his father's trade until he emerged as a charismatic rabbi in Galilee in the late 20s. Although taught to read and write Hebrew in the local synagogue school, his proficiency in the Hebrew Scriptures was largely acquired through private study. Jesus spoke Aramaic, the everyday language of the people, though he almost certainly also knew Greek, the common language of the eastern Mediterranean.

In 3 BC the local tetrarch ('ruler of a quarter') Herod Antipas established Sepphoris as his capital, a mere hour's walk from Nazareth. Perhaps Joseph and Jesus worked there during the rebuilding of the city in Antipas' early years. In AD 17, however, the tetrarch built a new capital on the lakeside, naming it Tiberias after the new emperor. The hamlets, villages and towns were organized regionally by a tight network of bureaucrats loyal to the ruler in Tiberias. A few wealthy grandees owned most of the land, with a majority of the population eking out their livelihoods as day labourers or fishermen.

Only in the previous century had the Jews reconquered and re-Judaized Galilee after five hundred years under pagan rule since the Babylonian invasion. By Jesus' day, however, there were active synagogues in every town and village. Yet this tiny northern principality was surrounded by paganism: Samaria to the south, Tyre and Sidon to the west and north, Gaulanitis to the north-east, and the Decapolis cities of Hippos, Gadara and Scythopolis to the east and south-east.

Galilee was a hotbed of religious extremism, notably exemplified in the warlord family of Ezekias and his son Judas the Galilean, who mounted a rebellion in AD 6 against the Roman occupation of Judea. It is probable that whole populations of some of the villages were descended from particular tribes. It has been suggested, for example, that Nazareth was composed of descendants of David who had settled there on return from the Babylonian exile.

As an observant Jew Jesus would have attended the synagogue on the sabbath and journeyed to Jerusalem for the major feasts, especially the Passover. Once Jesus crossed into Judea, however, he passed from Jewish to Roman jurisdiction. (The high priest and temple hierarchy merely acted as surrogates of the Romans in their day-to-day control of the holy city, Jerusalem.)

Jesus was approaching thirty when a series of crises erupted.

First, there was the arrival in AD 26 of a new prefect, to remain in office for more than a decade. Pontius Pilate was a lower-order military official who owed his appointment to the patronage of the sinister Praetorian Prefect L. Aelius Sejanus, who had become de facto emperor when Tiberius retired to Capri. Sejanus hated the Jews and it seems he sent Pilate to create trouble in Judea. Pilate, based in Caesarea Maritima, immediately stirred up hostility by bringing the Roman military standards bearing pagan effigies into Jerusalem, something never done before. Furthermore, he raided the sacred treasury in the temple to build an aqueduct and also minted coins with idolatrous symbols. Jesus' final arrival in Jerusalem at Passover AD 30 or 33 unfortunately almost coincided with a recent uprising led by Barabbas, something that may have prejudiced a brutal and corrupt governor against Jesus.

Secondly, in AD 28 the voice of a mighty prophet was raised in the land, after centuries of prophetic silence. Although the son of a priest, and therefore himself a priest, John the Baptist launched a powerful attack against the temple, the sacrifices and (by implication) the high priest, Caiaphas. John positioned himself on the far side of the Jordan in Perea in the jurisdiction of Herod Antipas, out of reach of the high priest and the Romans. There he preached that the people should come to *him* for baptism (signifying moral cleansing), confessing their sins. In other words, John was implying that the temple sacrifices were ineffective for securing forgiveness from God, but that God had ordained *his* baptism and preaching for that purpose. Furthermore, in addressing Jesus as the 'Lamb of God' who 'takes away the sin of the world', John was also implying that the temple sacrifices for sins had been superseded by the forthcoming death of the man Jesus (John 1:29).

John, however, rejected the suggestion that he was the Messiah, humbly asserting instead that he was merely preparing the way for the mightier one to come after him. John's anti-temple message, his declaration of this moment of time as divinely sanctioned, and his identification of Jesus as the Passover Lamb may have been important in Jesus' own identification of his identity and vocation as Messiah.

John, however, condemned his ruler, the tetrarch Herod Antipas, for his marriage to Herodias, the wife of Herod's half-brother Philip, something that was in breach of the Levitical teaching. For this, as well as for his popularity, of which the tetrarch was jealous, John was imprisoned in the fortress at Machaerus, east of the Dead Sea, where he was later executed at Herodias' request. John's removal was the signal for Jesus to appear and commence his public ministry.

That ministry appears to have occupied the years AD 29–33, although many believe the date should be AD 27–30. Either way, the period of ministry of three to four years is generally agreed.

Broadly speaking, Jesus' preaching and healing were focused on Galilee, with a brief period in the north and east and with his final weeks in Judea and Jerusalem. Twelve disciples accompanied him, to whom he explained both the inner meaning of the parables he delivered in public and the debates he engaged in with the scribes. He was arrested and tried by the high priest at the Passover in AD 30 or 33 and handed over to the Romans, who executed him for treason against the Roman emperor, though Pilate was unconvinced about the accusation. The four Gospels agree that the women found the burial tomb empty when they came there early on the first day of the week and that Jesus appeared alive to the disciples on a number of occasions over a thirty-seven-day period.

It is clear, therefore, that we have considerable information about Jesus, despite the passage of two thousand years. To illustrate the point, let us contrast Jesus with William Shakespeare, the world's greatest playwright, who has had a profound influence on the English language. A historian from the eighteenth century wrote that all we know of the great man is that he was born in Stratford-upon-Avon, fathered children there, travelled to London, where he became an actor and writer, and returned to Stratford where he died.[1] More recently, scholars have laboriously searched baptismal registers, loan records and other archives to fill out the picture, but William Shakespeare remains an elusive figure with few extra details known about him. True, we are aware of the times in which he lived and, of course, his brilliant writings. But the man remains in the shadows.

The times in which Jesus lived are also accessible to scholarship, and, as we know Shakespeare through his plays, we know the mind of Jesus through his teachings. Unlike Shakespeare, however, we know a lot about Jesus' whereabouts, actions and companions. This is the more remarkable since the events happened so long ago in a remote corner of the Roman Empire – and involved a Jew executed as a criminal, whose immediate followers were men of humble origin!

3. MESSIAH PROMISED

The longing for the coming of the Messiah burned brightly in the times of Jesus. Evidence for this yearning is found in two synagogue prayers from that era:

> Be gracious, O Lord, our God, according to your great mercies
> to Israel thy people,
> and Jerusalem your city,
> and Zion, residence of your glory;
> and to your temple and dwelling place;
> and to the kingdom of the house of David, *your righteous Messiah.*
>
> Make *the branch of David* soon spring forth,
> And let his horn be exalted by thy salvation.[1]

This sense of messianic awareness is also seen in the temple authorities' question to John the Baptist, 'Are you the Christ?' Furthermore, John himself later sent messengers to Jesus to ask if, after all, he was the 'One who was to come'? Clearly, urgent messianic hopes were current (John 1:20; Matt. 11:2).

This longing arose from prophetic oracles about a *coming king*, given many centuries before. The term 'Messiah' (Anointed One) was not used until after the Old Testament period and arose out of the expectation of a coming king, whom the Lord God had specifically *anointed*. God's act of anointing kings and priests in the Old Testament evolved into the idea of *the* Anointed One, an idea that had become strong in Israel for several centuries before the advent of Jesus of Nazareth.

The line of David

Two prophecies in particular became the basis for numerous later prophecies repeatedly replayed over many hundreds of years.

In the first, the aged patriarch Jacob before he died spoke to his twelve sons, with special reference to Judah, whom he called 'lion': 'The sceptre [royal staff] shall not depart from Judah . . .' (Gen. 49:10). From Judah's tribe was to come the royal line of kings, and Jacob promised the sceptre would not depart from this tribe.

The second oracle came a millennium later and was spoken by the prophet Nathan to young king David:

> When your days are fulfilled and you lie down with your fathers, I will raise up your offspring after you, who shall come forth from your body, and I will establish his kingdom. He shall build a house for my name, and I will establish the throne of his kingdom for ever. (2 Sam. 7:12–13)

Here God has narrowed the promise of the coming king from the tribe of Judah to a particular member of that tribe, to David and his descendants. In promising that the throne and kingdom of David's son will be *for ever*, the Lord is looking onwards beyond the king's immediate son, Solomon, to someone infinitely greater.

Psalm 2

Many of David's psalms reveal his sense of special calling to be God's anointed king, the Son of God (see e.g. Ps. 45:6–7).

In Psalm 2, which many attribute to David,[2] the nations conspire to cut the tie between God and his king, enthroned in Zion, Jerusalem:

> The kings of the earth set themselves,
>   and the rulers take counsel together,
>   against the LORD [God] and his anointed, saying,
> 'Let us burst their bonds asunder,
>   and cast their cords from us.'
> (v. 2)

But this conspiracy will fail. On the contrary, the anointed king, God's 'Son', will destroy the enemies of God and instead extend his kingdom to 'the ends of the earth' (v. 8). David concludes his psalm by warning the kings of the earth to be wise, and to embrace the Son. David is looking into the far distance, beyond the political circumstances of the moment.

The Assyrian menace: Isaiah and Micah

In the eighth century BC, Assyria (today's northern Iraq), the world superpower, threatened to engulf the smaller kingdoms to the south, including Judah and Israel. The two prophets who kept the messianic hopes alive were Isaiah and Micah.

Isaiah

By that time the formerly united kingdom of David had divided into the northern kingdom (called either Israel, Samaria or Ephraim) and the southern kingdom (Judah), whose capital was Jerusalem. The northern kingdom had a succession of capitals, notably Megiddo. In Jerusalem the king was Ahaz, from David's line, according to Nathan's promise to David.

The threat of invasion from Assyria forced Ephraim and Syria into a defensive alliance. In turn they attempted to coerce Judah to join them to form an alliance of three against the northern superpower. The two allies, however, had another motive. They sought to depose Ahaz and install a non-Davidic king in Jerusalem, thus overturning the promises of God (Isa. 7:5–6). Ahaz was terrified and torn between belief and unbelief about the intentions of the Lord. Nonetheless, although Ahaz 'wearied' the Lord because of his vacillations, he was promised a 'sign':

> Therefore the Lord himself will give you a sign.
> Behold, a young woman [virgin] shall conceive and bear a son,
> and shall call his name Immanuel.
> He shall eat curds and honey . . .
> (Isa. 7:14–15)[3]

In other words, God promised to sustain the line of David in Jerusalem by (1) a son, born of a virgin, (2) who was to be named Immanuel (God with us), but (3) (paradoxically) who would eat *poor* man's food of curdled milk and honey.

As with many of God's promises, the fulfilment was deferred, in this instance because of Ahaz's unbelief. Many centuries were to pass before Immanuel, born of a virgin, would come to claim the throne of David (Matt. 1:23; Luke 2:11–12).

Meanwhile, Assyria, like a swollen river, burst its banks and engulfed not only Syria and Ephraim, but Judah too (Isa. 7:17; 8:7–8). Yet the Lord gives other reassuring promises, now amazingly directed to Galilee, in the *northern* kingdom:

> In the former time he brought into contempt
> the land of Zebulun and the land of Naphtali,
> but in the latter time he will make glorious the way of the sea,
> the land beyond the Jordan, Galilee of the nations.
> (Isa. 9:1; Matt. 4:15–16)

To *Galilee* of the nations God promises a son to rule for ever on the throne of David:

> For to us a child is born,
>   to us a son is given;
> and the government will be upon his shoulder,
>   and his name will be called

'Wonderful Counsellor, Mighty God, Everlasting Father, Prince of
   Peace.'
Of the increase of his government and of peace
   there will be no end,
upon the throne of David, and over his kingdom,
   to establish it, and to uphold it
with justice and with righteousness
   from this time forth and for evermore.
(Isa. 9:6–7; Luke 2:11; 1:32–33)

A great light will shine in Galilee through the *Son* the Lord will
send, whom he calls 'mighty God', who will rule upon David's
throne and whose righteous kingdom will be for *evermore*.

By contrast, however, Assyria's dominance will be short-lived.
And from Assyria's scourge the Lord will restore a faithful
remnant (Isa. 11:15–16). On that great day the people of David's
city will 'sing and shout for joy', for great among them will be 'the
Holy One of Israel' (Isa. 12:6).

Finally, Isaiah is moved by God to prophesy about a son of
David upon whom the Spirit of the Lord will rest:

There shall come forth a shoot
   from the stump of Jesse,
and a branch shall grow out of his roots.
And the Spirit of the LORD shall rest upon him,
the spirit of wisdom and understanding,
the spirit of counsel and might,
the spirit of knowledge and the fear of the LORD.
(Isa. 11:1–2)

This king (whom Isaiah calls 'branch') will be righteous and dis-
cerning, will judge on behalf of the meek but oppose and destroy
the wicked:

And his delight shall be in the fear of the LORD.

He shall not judge by what his eyes see,
   or decide by what his ears hear;

> but with righteousness he shall judge the poor,
>> and decide with equity for the meek of the earth;
> and he shall smite the earth with the rod of his mouth,
>> and with the breath of his lips he shall slay the wicked.
>
> (Isa. 11:3–5)

Isaiah expresses these hopes in terms that transcend the politics of his time. This son of Jesse will be a world ruler who will usher in a new age, the end-time kingdom of God – in fact, nothing less than a reversal of the evils that flow from the disobedience of the primeval parents and the return, instead, to the blessings of the Garden of Eden:

> The wolf shall dwell with the lamb,
>> and the leopard shall lie down with the kid,
> and the calf and the lion and the fatling together,
>> and a little child shall lead them.
> The cow and the bear shall feed;
>> their young shall lie down together;
>> and the lion shall eat straw like the ox.
> The sucking child shall play over the hole of the asp,
>> and the weaned child shall put his hand on the adder's den.
> They shall not hurt or destroy
>> in all my holy mountain;
> for the earth shall be full of the knowledge of the LORD
>> as the waters cover the sea.

> In that day the root of Jesse shall stand as an ensign to the peoples;
> him shall the nations seek, and his dwellings shall be glorious.
>
> (Isa. 11:6–9)

This is remarkable. Isaiah begins by addressing the horrors of the Assyrian invasion, but ends by promising a righteous ruler descended from David who will rule the nations of the world in a kingdom that will reinstate the blessings of Eden lost by Adam and Eve's rebellion. These hopes were never realized in Isaiah's lifetime.

Micah

Micah, like Isaiah, prophesied to the people of Judah during Assyria's era of dominance, when Jothan, Ahaz and Hezekiah occupied David's royal throne in Jerusalem. Despite huge problems, Micah also held out hope for a continuing ruler in the line of David. He prophesied the birth of a king, from the tiny village of Bethlehem, David's birthplace:

> But you, O Bethlehem Ephrathah,
>   who are little to be among the clans of Judah,
> from you shall come forth for me
>   one who is to be ruler in Israel,
> whose origin is from of old,
>   from ancient days . . .
> And he shall stand and feed his flock in the strength of the LORD,
>   in the majesty of the name of the LORD his God.
> And they shall dwell secure, for now he shall be great
>   to the ends of the earth.
> (Mic. 5:2, 4; Matt. 2:6)

According to Micah, another shepherd-king will arise from the village of David, who will be 'great to the ends of the earth'. Once again a prophet speaks of an immediate hope that, however, was not fulfilled at that time but had to await the passage of many centuries for its promises to be realized.

In brief, then, despite the awesome threat to tiny Judah and its royal city, Jerusalem, the prophets Isaiah and Micah staunchly reiterate God's promises to Judah and David that a member of David's line will rule over God's kingdom for ever.

The Babylonian menace

By the sixth century BC the Assyrian Empire had fallen, to be replaced by the Babylonian Empire (modern-day Iraq). The little kingdoms of Israel and Judah again faced another superpower, poised to invade their countries and deport the people and, above all, to destroy the covenantal faith.

Jeremiah

Against this menace God raises up Jeremiah, who, like Isaiah, insists that the divine plans continue to be centred on Jerusalem, ruled by a descendant of David:

> Behold, the days are coming, says the LORD,
> when I will raise up for David a righteous Branch,
> and he shall reign as king and deal wisely,
> and shall execute justice and righteousness in the land.
> In his days Judah will be saved,
> and Israel will dwell securely.
> And this is the name by which he will be called:
> 'The LORD is our righteousness.'
> (Jer. 23:5–6)

Jeremiah foresees that the Babylonians will conquer Jerusalem and carry off her leaders to the land of the two rivers. He, like Isaiah, prophesies that the Lord will bring them back to their homeland, as if in a new exodus:

> Therefore, behold, the days are coming, says the LORD,
>   when men shall no longer say,
> 'As the LORD lives
> who brought up the people of Israel out of the land of Egypt,'
>   but 'As the LORD lives
> who brought up and led the descendants of the house of Israel
> out of the north country
> and out of all the countries where he had driven them.'
> Then they shall dwell in their own land.
> (Jer. 23:7–8)

Events play out according to Jeremiah's prophecies. The Babylonians take the people into captivity but after a period return to their own land. Yet the hope of a Davidic ruler is not realized in the short term.

Ezekiel

Ezekiel, along with many leaders from Jerusalem, is carried off captive to Babylon. There he addresses the people as the poor lost sheep scattered far from their true homeland. The Lord through Ezekiel promises a new David, a shepherd-king to rescue his people and bring them home:

> And I will set up over them one shepherd, my servant David,
> and he shall feed them: he shall feed them and be their shepherd.
> (Ezek. 34:23)

After seventy years the people are able to return to Judah, but where is the shepherd-king, David? Once again we notice a promise unfulfilled around the time the prophecy is given.

From this brief survey covering the period from the eighth to sixth centuries we observe that, despite repeated crises over several centuries from the mighty empires of the Assyrians and the Babylonians, God sustained the hopes of his people through the voice of the prophets Isaiah, Micah, Jeremiah and Ezekiel.

The Persian era

By the fifth century BC the Persians have defeated the Babylonians. The people of Israel and Judah now serve a new master, the Persians. The former kingdoms of Judah and Israel are now minor provinces (called 'satrapies') on the edges of the sprawling Persian kingdom. Surely this will spell the end of the kingdom of Judah and the line of David?

Zechariah

Once more, however, God raises up a prophet, Zechariah. And rather than diminishing the hope of a Davidic king ruling in Jerusalem this prophet actually expands it. In fact, Zechariah has more to say about Jerusalem and the royal line than any other prophet.

He calls the hoped-for son of David 'the Branch', based on Isaiah's prophecy of 'the branch' that will grow out of Jesse's roots (11:1), a point repeated by Jeremiah (23:5): 'Hear now, O Joshua the high priest, you and your friends who sit before you . . . behold, I will bring my servant *the Branch*' (Zech. 3:8).

This messianic 'Branch' will also be a priest who will build a new temple for the Lord:

> Thus says the LORD of hosts,
> 'Behold, the man whose name is *the Branch* . . .
> shall build the temple of the LORD,
> and shall bear royal honour,
> and shall sit and rule upon his throne.'
> (Zech. 6:12–13)

In the following four oracles Zechariah prophesies that the Lord will dwell in Jerusalem, which will become the place of goodness and peace, to which the saved remnant will return:

> Thus says the LORD:
> I will return to Zion, and will dwell in the midst of Jerusalem,
> and Jerusalem shall be called the faithful city,
> and the mountain of the LORD of hosts, the holy mountain.

> Thus says the LORD of hosts:
> Old men and old women shall again sit in the streets of Jerusalem,
> each with staff in hand for very age.
> And the streets of the city shall be full of boys and girls playing in its
>   streets.

> Thus says the LORD of hosts:
> If it is marvellous in the sight of the remnant of this people in these
>   days, should it also be marvellous in my sight, says the LORD of hosts?

> Thus says the LORD˙ of hosts:
> Behold, I will save my people from the east country
> and from the west country;
> and I will bring them to dwell in the midst of Jerusalem;

and they shall be my people and I will be their God,
in faithfulness and in righteousness.
(Zech. 8:3–8)

Furthermore, even the nations of the world will stream into
Jerusalem to find salvation there:

Many peoples and strong nations
shall come to seek the LORD of hosts in Jerusalem,
and to entreat the favour of the LORD.
Thus says the LORD of hosts:
In those days ten men from the nations of every tongue
shall take hold of the robe of a Jew, saying,
'Let us go with you, for we have heard that God is with you.'
(Zech. 8:22–23)

When Jerusalem's triumphant but humble king comes, who will
rule the nations, a time of world peace will prevail:

Rejoice greatly, O daughter of Zion!
    Shout aloud, O daughter of Jerusalem!
Lo, your king comes to you;
    triumphant and victorious is he,
humble and riding on an ass,
    on a colt the foal of an ass.
I will cut off the chariot from Ephraim
    and the warhorse from Jerusalem;
and the battle bow shall be cut off,
    and he shall command peace to the nations;
his dominion shall be from sea to sea,
    and from the River to the ends of the earth.
(Zech. 9:9–10)

Like many such prophecies, this one did not find fulfilment at the
time Zechariah spoke.

Remarkably, however, despite the achievements of this king, the
house of David and the people of Jerusalem will 'pierce' him, and
then mourn his death:

And I will pour out on the house of David and the inhabitants of
   Jerusalem
a spirit of compassion and supplication,
so that, when they look on him whom *they* have pierced,
they shall mourn for him, as one mourns for an only child,
and weep bitterly over him, as one weeps over a first-born.
(Zech. 12:10)

Zechariah reveals that the 'pierced' one will actually be God's
shepherd-king:

'Awake, O sword, against my shepherd,
   against the man who stands next to me,' says the LORD of hosts.
'Strike the shepherd, that the sheep may be scattered;
   I will turn my hand against the little ones'.
(Zech. 13:7)

According to Zechariah, God will bring a new David as shepherd-king to his restored city, Jerusalem, which will become a place
of divine blessing for the nations of the world. Yet members of
his own house will 'pierce' and 'strike' down this 'David'. These
prophecies were not fulfilled in Zechariah's time.

The nature of Old Testament prophecy

This brief survey reveals an unusual characteristic of prophecy
in the Old Testament: the prophets spoke out of a specific situation of need, often with the expectation of an immediate
fulfilment, but equally often a fulfilment beyond the horizon of
hope. The distant and transcendent and the immediate and
mundane were typically connected, as if there were no expanse
of time separating them. The prophet did not distinguish
between the immediate and distant future. It was the same word
of the Lord and the outcome of both was the work of the same
God.

   In effect, this means we read the prophets with one eye on their
immediate political situation but the other on their God-given

insight into the longer-term future. It was that more distant future about the Davidic King, Jerusalem and the nations that engaged Jesus of Nazareth.

The long-term promises

The time span between Jacob's promise to Judah and Zechariah's prophecies is about thirteen centuries. It emerges from this brief survey covering many centuries that the Lord promised and reiterated his assurances that Judah was his chosen tribe, David's his elect 'house' and Jerusalem his uniquely special dwelling place. Despite the bleak circumstances created by a succession of hostile kingdoms (Assyria, Babylon and Persia) God raised up prophet after prophet to keep alive the hopes of the people. Clearly, however, the prophets began to project these David- and Jerusalem-centred hopes in ways that transcended the political circumstances of their respective days.

This is a list of the principal elements of the prophecies of God's anointed king:

1. He will belong to the tribe of Judah and be a descendant of King David (Gen. 49:10; 2 Sam. 7:13).
2. He will defeat his enemies and his kingdom will extend to the ends of the earth (Ps. 2:8; Isa. 11:4, 9–10).
3. He will be born of a virgin, be called Immanuel and be poor (Isa. 7:14–15).
4. He will be called 'mighty God . . . prince of peace' and bring the light of God to the Gentiles (Isa. 9:2, 6).
5. His light will dawn in Galilee and he will rule for ever (Isa. 9:1, 7).
6. The Spirit of the Lord will rest upon him (Isa. 11:2).
7. He will be born in Bethlehem (Mic. 5:4).
8. He will be wise and righteous, merciful to the meek (Isa. 11:2–3; Jer. 5 – 6).
9. He will be a shepherd-king ruling a united people (Ezek. 34:23–34).
10. He will be a priest-king, a peacemaker who will enter Jerusalem

triumphantly but humbly, riding on a young donkey, and his
kingdom will be universal (Zech. 8:4–8; 9:9–10).

11. He will be 'pierced', 'struck down' and killed (Zech.
12:10; 13:7).

Interpretations of the Messiah promises

When the voice of the prophets fell silent (in the fourth century
BC), the hope for the Messiah continued.[4] A devout Jew who took
the pseudonym Ezra wrote symbolically of a 'lion' (the Messiah)
who would serve God against an 'eagle', an enemy of God.
Clearly, this 'Ezra' was picking up Jacob's words to Judah in
Genesis 49:9–10.

> As for the *lion* whom you saw . . . speaking to the eagle
> and reproving him for his unrighteousness and all his deeds,
> as you have heard:
>
> This is the *Messiah* whom the Most High has kept to the end of days,
> who shall spring from the seed of *David*.
> (*4 Ezra* 12.31–32)[5]

Another devout Jew took the pseudonym 'Solomon' and composed a number of 'psalms' about two hundred years before Jesus
began preaching. This anonymous writer was disillusioned with
the Maccabean rulers who had expelled the Gentile occupation
only to be corrupted by the ways of the Gentiles. So the writer
pleads with God to at last send the Messiah from the line of
David. He bases his poem on Psalm 2:

> Behold, O Lord, and raise up for them their king, the *son of David* . . .
> And gird him with strength, that he may shatter unrighteous rulers . . .
> With a rod of iron he shall break in pieces all their substance . . .
> And there shall be no unrighteousness in his days in their midst,
> for all shall be holy and their king shall be the *anointed* [the Messiah]
> of the Lord . . .
> (*Psalms of Solomon* 17.23, 36)[6]

The physical violence of this 'psalm' is even more explicit in a later prayer:

> How beautiful is the *king Messiah*,
> who will arise from those who are of the house of Judah.
> He goes forth and orders the battle array against his enemies
> and slays kings along with their overlords,
> and no king or overlord can stand before him;
> he reddens the mountains with the blood of the slain,
> his clothing is dipped in blood like a winepress.
> (*Palestinian Targum*, Gen. 49:10)[7]

This Messiah is a warrior-king who will be reddened with the blood of his enemies.

The hoped for Messiah in these texts from the general era of Jesus is based on only one or two of the many aspects of the Messiah from prophets as noted above. Understandably, times of great disappointment about the Maccabean and Herodian rulers evoked nationalistic hopes of a king like the bloodied warrior David, who defeated his enemies.

But these interpretations ignore, for example, those prophecies about the Messiah's deity ('Immanuel', 'mighty God'), humility, peacemaking and his violent death that are so prominent in the prophetic writings, also as noted above.

When *all* the jigsaw pieces are considered and assembled, we begin to see how they are globally fulfilled in Jesus of Nazareth. Indeed, at Caesarea Philippi the disciples through Peter specifically identify Jesus as the Christ (Messiah). Jesus says that recognition is the 'rock' on which he will erect his church; that is, the new temple as prophesied (2 Sam. 7:13; Zech. 6:13; cf. Matt. 16:16–18). He was, indeed, of the line of David, Immanuel, 'mighty God' and the 'prince of peace', but who was 'pierced' and 'struck down'.

Several puzzling aspects of these prophecies, however, do not appear to be fulfilled in Jesus, at least not in the short term. One is that Jesus, who was 'meek and gentle', did not pursue the military activities of the Messiah (Ps. 2:8; Isa. 11:4). Another is that since Jerusalem rejected this new 'David', it is unclear how the holy city will have the significant place heralded by the prophets.

Broadly speaking, the answer is in Jesus' attitude to himself as the fulfilment of the prophets *within* history and his attitude to the ultimate fulfilment of the prophets *at the end of* history. *Within history* Jesus saw himself as fulfilling the hopes of the prophets, which he interpreted in terms of the Messiah's humility in service of others and humiliation in death as a ransom for many. Here Jesus joined the messianic prophecies noted above *and* those of the suffering servant of Isaiah 52 – 53. He was the Servant-Messiah, who was at the same time humble *and* majestic.

At the end of history Jesus foresaw the final and absolute judgment of the nations, which would depend on their welcome or rejection of those who came to them in Jesus' name. For to welcome these messengers was to welcome Jesus, and to reject them was to reject him. Christ will sit on his throne as judge and separate the people of the nations as a shepherd separates sheep from goats (Matt. 25:31–46). He will consign his enemies to the eternal fire, thus fulfilling the warrior-Messiah prophecies of Psalm 2:8 and Isaiah 11:4.

In regard to Jerusalem, Jesus prophesied the destruction and also the rebuilding of the temple, but makes no precise reference to a new Jerusalem (Mark 13:2 par.; John 2:19; Matt. 16:18). However, a strong tradition of a *new* Jerusalem is evident in the New Testament. Paul speaks of a Jerusalem 'that is above', the letter to the Hebrews of a 'heavenly Jerusalem' and Revelation of the 'new Jerusalem' (Gal. 4:26; Heb. 12:22; Rev. 3:12; 21:2, 10). Probably, these writers echo teachings they know are consistent with those of Jesus.

Jesus' prophecy and Old Testament prophecy

In the latter part of his ministry Jesus repeatedly referred to himself as a heavenly ruler, *the* Son of Man, but also (paradoxically) as the humiliated Servant of the Lord who would bear the sins of many (e.g. Mark 10:45; cf. Dan. 7:13–14; Isa. 53:12; Zech. 12:10). When he eventually reached Jerusalem, it was not as a David-like warrior come to raise up the armies of God to expel the Romans and extend God's kingdom to the ends of the earth, but rather as the humble Messiah, a servant of the people.

In Jerusalem Jesus identified himself as 'the Christ' by *word* (to the people in the temple and to the high priest; Mark 12:35; 14:62) and *action* (riding up to and cleansing the temple in the manner predicted by Zechariah; Zech. 9:9; 14:21; Mark 11:1–10, 15–19). He powerfully lifted Messiah to a higher plane by indicating that the Anointed One was actually not so much David's 'son' as David's 'Lord', seated in authority at the right hand of God (Mark 12:35–37; Ps. 110:1). Furthermore, he pointed to himself as not merely part of the succession of prophets, but as the beloved Son, sent by God to Israel, thereby fulfilling Isaiah's prophecy of a son (Mark 12:6; Isa. 7:14; 9:6).

The situation, then, is that Jesus saw the great messianic prophecies converging on himself, yet differently and in such a way that by his life, death and resurrection he *inaugurated* processes and released spiritual forces that would eventuate in the final, universal and absolute fulfilment of those ancient prophecies. In Jesus we see both the end of the beginning and the beginning of the end.

This will satisfactorily explain why, after his death and resurrection, he was immediately worshipped and proclaimed. The key to understanding Jesus is that he saw himself as the human point at which the promises and prophecies of God converged and from whom they were projected forward into the ultimate future.

It is the stumbling stone for all 'liberal' and sectarian views of Christ that they do not credibly address Jesus' high view of himself *in terms of the promises of the prophets*. Whether it is Geza Vermes's 'Jewish' Jesus or John Dominic Crossan's 'Greek' Jesus (see chapter 2), in neither case is Jesus' engagement with prophecy taken seriously. Their alternative is to assert that such engagement is not historically authentic, but has been imposed on Jesus after the event by the early church.

There are several problems with this explanation. One is to ask why it would have occurred to his followers to make a mere rabbi or prophet into something he was not. Numbers of impressive rabbis and charismatic leaders were active in that era, yet *none* was accorded messianic status after death. Related is the observation that great minds produce powerful thoughts and that committees do not. It is more satisfying to believe that Jesus was that 'great mind' who drew these prophecies together, rather than that the 'committee' of the early church did so.

4. MESSIAH WORSHIPPED

It is a secure fact of history that after the Romans crucified Jesus of Nazareth circa AD 33, his followers met weekly to worship him as Lord.

Worship of Christ, 'as if to a god'

Pliny, governor of the Roman Black Sea province of Bithynia, reported to the emperor Trajan early in the second century that the Christians met on a 'fixed day of the week' and chanted hymns to Christ 'as if to a god' (*Epistles* 10.96).[1] Pliny's friend the historian Tacitus, governor of the adjoining province of Roman Asia, wrote that Pontius Pilate had executed Christ during the reign of the emperor Tiberius.

These two famous Romans were quite negative about the new movement, which they regarded as a spreading disease. Between them, however, they not only tell us where and when the Romans executed Christ (in Judea, between 26 and 36), but also that his movement had grown worryingly and its members were expressing worship to this executed criminal 'as if to a god'.

These hostile Romans helpfully confirm the picture we have from the letters Paul and others wrote to Christian assemblies half a century earlier, within the time band 50–65. In a circular letter he wrote to a number of churches, Paul said that when they met they were to sing and make melody in their hearts '*to* the Lord' (Eph. 5:19; also 1 Cor. 14:26). Paul's churches were in Greek-speaking regions, but they had come to know some Semitic words that went back a couple of decades earlier to Jesus and to the time immediately after him in Palestine. One example is the word *abba*, an Aramaic word small children (as well as adults) would use for 'father' (Rom. 8:15; Gal. 4:6). Another example, and more to the point, is in the words of the prayer *Maran atha*, which mean, 'Lord, come back' (1 Cor. 16:22; also Rev. 22:20). It is evident, therefore, that the early Christians worshipped Jesus as Lord and prayed *to* him, pleading with him to return.

Jews like Paul worshipping *someone else*!

The breathtaking thing here is that Paul and most other writers in the New Testament were Jews. Paul, however, was no merely marginal or uninstructed Jew, but a leading younger Pharisee and a member of the prestigious academy of Gamaliel, the most famous rabbi of his day. A Jew like Paul would recite three times daily his nation's creed, 'Hear, O Israel: The LORD our God, the LORD is one' (Deut. 6:4). Moreover, none knew better than he that the Commandments forbade worshipping any person or thing instead of, or as well as, the Lord.

Yet here is Pharisee-trained Paul, who never renounced his Jewishness (Rom. 9:1–5; 2 Cor. 11:22), committing the greatest of sins for a Jew: worshipping someone alongside God. More even than this, Paul the Jew had come to redefine God as Jesus' *Father* so that Jesus was the *Son* of this Father. In calling Jesus *Lord*, Paul was identifying the risen and ascended Jesus with the Lord of the Old Testament. This is clear from Paul's words, which echo but radically adapt the Jewish creed quoted above: 'There is *one* God, the Father . . . and *one* Lord, Jesus Christ' (1 Cor. 8:6). The *one* Lord of his Jewish faith Paul now redefined as the *one* Father and the *one* Lord.

Doubting the pre-crucifixion Jesus

Why did Paul undergo such an intellectual revolution? Only one answer is possible: Jesus' impact upon Paul.

Paul is not alone in this worshipful attitude to Jesus. In fact, every contributor to our New Testament calls Jesus 'Christ' and 'Lord'. And they are all Jews except Luke, a Jew in all but name, since he was probably a God-fearer, a non-Jew who believed in Israel's Lord and attended the synagogue.

What I write here is historical fact no serious scholar doubts. The writings of Pliny, Tacitus and Paul are securely dated and rest on well-attested manuscripts. Moreover, they are commentary on living situations and are not written to prove or disprove the history of early Christianity.

The thing many serious scholars do doubt, however, is that the historical figure of Jesus was potentially worshipful. In fact, the general assumption of many is that in their worship of Jesus in the years after him, the early Christians were grievously mistaken. Such scholars say that the historical Jesus must have been *something other* than the early Christians had come to believe and worship. The blame for this mistake is usually attributed to Paul; which is unfair, since *all* the letter writers in the New Testament teach that the post-resurrection Jesus is *Lord*, to be worshipped, served and obeyed.

Those scholars who claim that Jesus was something other usually engage in what has been called 'nothing buttery'. The real Jesus, they say, was *nothing but* x, y or z, in fact, *anything but* a figure to be worshipped. It is not that they attribute evil to him, although some have: Morton Smith, for example, said he was a wicked magician.[2]

One scholar who views Jesus positively is Geza Vermes, who mounted a case that Jesus was a 'charismatic' rabbi whose prayers God answered in amazing ways. Vermes, an expert on the Dead Sea

Scrolls and other Jewish literature, found parallels to Jesus in the rabbis Honi the Circle Drawer (also known as Onias) and Hanina ben Dosa.[3] Honi lived more than a century before Jesus, and Hanina some decades after. Both were holy men and Hanina is credited with several miracles through answered prayer. Neither Honi nor Hanina had messianic claims made for them, nor seem to have had any sense of mission to Israel. Few scholars have followed Vermes's attempt to find similarities between these rabbis and Jesus.

Also positive about Jesus is John Dominic Crossan, who seeks to explain Jesus as a Galilean social subversive who had been influenced by the Greek Cynic movement,[4] and who was seeking to overturn the corrupt, powerful and property-owning elites in the rural areas.[5] According to Crossan, Jesus' agenda is represented in certain early (wisdom) strands of the so-called Q source underlying Matthew and Luke, but also in the second-century *Gospel of Thomas* (see chapter 17). Crossan holds that Jesus' simple and direct message was subsequently corrupted in Jerusalem by Mark and later by Paul. Most of the New Testament according to Crossan has been corrupted and is quite *unlike* the simplicity and goodness of Jesus' true message.

It is no exaggeration to say that hundreds of Jesus books have been written in recent years. Those by Vermes and Crossan are only two, the former presenting a Jewish Jesus and the latter a Greek-influenced Jesus. The one important thing they, and most other books about Jesus, have in common is their assertion that Jesus was *nothing but* a rabbi, prophet or reformer. Implicit or explicit, therefore, is their assumption of *discontinuity* between the historical, pre-resurrection Jesus and the post-resurrection figure whom the early Christians worshipped.

Flawed reasoning

To drive this wedge between *their* Jesus and the early church's worshipped Christ they must do several things. First, they avoid referring to the chronological closeness between the end of Jesus' lifespan and the beginning of the church's worship of him as Lord and Christ. In remaining silent about chronological closeness, they imply that these developments occurred over many decades or even centuries. Paul, however, penned the prayer *Maran atha* in circa 54, a mere two decades later than Jesus. But the Semitic language identifies the words as a prayer written in Palestine from earlier times, arguably much earlier times, going back almost to the time of Jesus. That, certainly, must be the view we take of the origin of the word *abba*. In fact, Paul identified much of the teaching about Christ in his letters as crafted by others before him. Think for example of his reminder about the Last Supper, where the instructions go back to Jesus and the 'night he was betrayed', or his reminder to the church in Corinth about the details of Christ's death and resurrection sightings (1 Cor. 11:23–26; 15:3–5). These speak of chronological closeness between Jesus and Paul, a point not noticed by those for whom Jesus must have been *something other*.

Secondly, they provide no cogent explanation why Paul attempted to destroy early Christianity (1 Cor. 15:9; Gal. 1:13, 23; Phil. 3:6). Once more, chronology is important, since the young Pharisee attacked the church very early in its life, perhaps only a matter of months after the first Easter. The 'sect of the Nazarenes', as it was called, was but one of a number of subgroups within Judaism. The Jewish historian and propagandist Josephus mentions 'four philosophies' among the Jews at that time: Pharisees, Saduccees, Essenes and Religious Revolutionaries. Paul the Pharisee, for example, did not attack the Essenes. There was but one reason why he attacked the early Christians: in their preaching about Jesus as Messiah, they at the same time denied pillars of Judaism, such as the temple and the law. Paul understood well Jesus had made temple and law irrelevant. For the young Pharisee, Jesus was a pseudo-messiah who undercut the pillars of the Jewish faith.

Thirdly, those who drive a wedge between the historical Jesus and the historical worshipping church frequently ignore or seriously diminish the usefulness of the Acts of the Apostles. This book is the second volume to the Gospel of Luke, a work that narrates the life and ministry of Jesus from his birth to his death and resurrection. At the beginning of the second book, the Acts of the

Apostles, Peter declared that 'God has made him both Lord and Christ, *this Jesus* whom you crucified' (Acts 2:36). In other words, Luke the author of the Gospel and the Acts allows us to hear from Peter the *continuity* between the pre-crucified Jesus and the post-Easter One, whom he now declares to be the object of worship and obedience.

The book of Acts plays a critical role in the New Testament, since it serves as a bridge between the pre-crucified Jesus and early Christianity. Yet in the indexes to his book *The Birth of Christianity* Crossan does not have even one reference to the Acts of the Apostles. According to him the decades after Jesus are 'dark ages . . . cloaked in silence'.[6] This is, of course, nonsense. Paul's letter to the Galatians, which Crossan does not dispute, has extensive information about the period immediately after Jesus, information that corroborates the Acts of the Apostles at many points.[7]

At the beginning of Luke-Acts the author claims his two books are dependent on written sources handed to him by those who were from the beginning 'eyewitnesses' (of Jesus) and 'ministers of the word' (the original disciples-become-apostles). To disregard Luke-Acts and its account of the continuity between the pre-crucifixion Jesus and the proclamation of Christ after Easter by the apostles is, in effect, to call into question the integrity of this author. This is an unsustainable option, however, since again and again by cross-checking he can be shown to be observant, competent and honest. Moreover, and not of least importance, this Luke was the devoted companion of Paul who tells us that he stayed with Peter for two weeks in Jerusalem, where he also met James, the brother of Jesus (Gal. 1:18–19). Through his friend Paul, Luke had excellent second-hand information about Peter and James, the leaders of early Christianity, who were there at the birth of the church in Jerusalem, immediately after the lifespan of Jesus of Nazareth. The Acts is the bridge between Jesus and the early church, without which we would not be able to understand the origins of Christianity.

The logic of history

To engage in *nothing buttery* about the pre-crucifixion Jesus is to run away from the logic of history. Since *immediately after* Jesus' death his followers proclaimed him to be Messiah and Lord, prayed *to* him to 'come back', and sang hymns *to* him, we cannot escape reality by diminishing and redefining him as *nothing but* a rabbi or prophet or reformer or some other lesser figure. Simple historical cause-and-effect considerations and chronological closeness demand other answers about the identity and mission of *this Jesus*. This is not a matter of unthinking dogma or blind faith (of which Christians are sometimes guilty), but of hard facts and inescapable reality. There must have been something very substantial about the pre-crucifixion Jesus to establish the trajectory of continuity that proceeded so quickly into early Christianity. Long ago Johannes Weiss asked, 'How could belief in [Jesus'] Messiahship emerge as an entirely new phenomenon if he himself had not provided the impulse for it?'[8] On grounds of historical probability, the idea that Jesus was the Messiah must have derived from Jesus himself.

5. MESSIAH RECOGNIZED

The whole point of the Gospel of Mark is to demonstrate that Jesus was the Messiah. Mark wrote his Gospel in Greek, where the Hebrew words for 'the Messiah' are translated as 'the Christ'. His opening words summarize all that will follow: 'The beginning of the gospel of Jesus [the] Christ, the Son of God'.

The dramatic midpoint of this Gospel comes when Jesus challenges his followers to declare who *they* believe him to be. Peter memorably answers for the other disciples, 'You are the Christ' (Mark 8:29).

Jesus immediately leads them from Caesarea Philippi, in the extreme north, to Jerusalem, in the south, where he provocatively rides up to the City of David in the manner the Messiah was expected to arrive (Mark 11:1–11; Zech. 9:9). Some time later he drives out the traders and moneychangers from the temple precincts, referring to it as 'a den of robbers', whereas God intends it to be 'a house of prayer for all nations' (Mark 11:17).[1] These are two calculated messianic acts, in line with prophecies about the coming Messiah, which reveal Jesus' hitherto unspoken conviction that he is the Messiah.

Events quickly take their inevitable course. The temple authorities demand to know by 'what authority' Jesus takes these dramatic actions, and then, upon his arrest, ask him directly, 'Are you the Christ, the Son of the Blessed?' Jesus seals his own fate by replying, 'I am' (Mark 14:61–62).

From Mark's Gospel, then, we learn that Peter and the disciples regarded Jesus as the Christ, and that Jesus himself believed himself to be the Christ, but that he did not make that claim public until he came to Jerusalem for the last time. There was a reason for this, as we shall see.

The temple hierarchy saw in Jesus' messianic claims a threat to their power. Had he been mad or an eccentric his worst fate would have been a severe flogging.[2] Clearly, though, he was neither mad nor eccentric but a credible and formidable figure who exercised remarkable influence over the ordinary people. Claims for his messianic status were credible.

Since only the Roman governor was authorized to execute capital punishment, the chief priests accused Jesus before the governor on the political charge of treason, that is, that Jesus of Nazareth claimed to be 'king of the Jews' (Mark 11:26). The Romans would have been mystified by the religious term 'Messiah', but were in no doubt about the meaning of the claim to be 'king of the Jews', since there was only one such king, the emperor Tiberius in Rome. Pilate appears to have been unconvinced that the man accused before him represented any threat to the *Pax Romana*, but yielded eventually to the pressure of the temple leaders.

In brief, then, the Gospel of Mark means us to understand that Jesus believed himself to be the long-awaited Messiah, the rightful God-appointed ruler of Israel, and for that conviction was executed for treason by the Roman provincial authorities.

Names as evidence

Several names provide evidence of Jesus as Messiah.

Simon the rock

It is beyond dispute that Jesus renamed Simon Bar-jona as Cephas (Greek, *Petros*; Mark 1:16; 3:16; John 1:42; cf. 21:15–17; Matt. 16:16–20).The names Cephas and Petros both mean 'rock' in their respective languages. In the coming years Paul consistently refers to this Simon by the Aramaic name Cephas (1 Cor. 1:12; 3:22; 9:5; 15:5; Gal. 1:18; 2:9, 11, 14) and calls him by the Greek name Petros only in passages where he has already used the name Cephas (Gal. 2:7–8). Jesus' renaming of Simon as Cephas must be regarded as historical.

Why did Jesus rename this man Cephas or 'rock'? Because Simon Bar-jona formally recognized the pre-crucifixion Jesus as Messiah (Matt. 16:16–20; Mark 8:29; John 1:42; 6:69). That is to say, Peter recognized that the lines of Old Testament prophecy converged on Jesus.

Furthermore, Cephas was the first (male) witness of the risen Christ (1 Cor. 15:5) and the leader of the initial mission (Greek, *apostolē*) to the Jews in Israel (Gal. 2:9). The persistent continuity of the new name and his recorded witness to the resurrection of the Messiah in Palestine is consistent with his pre-crucifixion recognition of Jesus' true identity as 'the Christ' (Acts 2 – 10 *passim*). Simon's new name Cephas, used both before and after the crucifixion, is testimony to his confession of Jesus as Messiah before the crucifixion.

'Messiahmen' in Antioch

In Antioch in Syria 'the disciples were for the first time called Christians' (Greek, *Christianoi*; Acts 11:26).[3] This was probably no later than the middle to late thirties, a mere five or six years after the crucifixion. Luke leaves unanswered the questions 'Who gave the disciples that name, and when was it given?' Scholars are probably correct in thinking that the name came from Roman administrators.[4] At this early stage *Christos* was not yet a surname but a title, so that the *Christianoi* were so called because they were followers of *the Christos*. Thus it sounds as if *Christianos was* the official term for a member of the new movement in the Syrian capital. Their members belonged to something unheard of, a group where Jews mixed with Gentiles, whose *raison d'être* was their mutual adherence to *the Christos*.

The intriguing question is whether or not the authorities in Antioch identified the movement as having its roots in Jerusalem. This is by no means improbable. Judea was a subsidiary of Antioch, Rome's chief eastern outpost, whose legions often had to march south to Judea in times of trouble. Pilate's execution in Jerusalem of a 'king of the Jews' may have come to the attention of his superior, the Roman military governor in Antioch. Furthermore, this Christian movement had been launched in Antioch by Jewish émigrés who had arrived from Jerusalem in recent times. The Roman administrators in Antioch probably identified the local *Christianoi* as having originated in Jerusalem with the one Pilate had crucified as 'king of the Jews'.

To summarize, the renaming of Simon as Cephas because he addressed Jesus as the Christ and the early naming of the *Christianoi* in Antioch are circumstantial evidence that Jesus was regarded as the Christ and that the Romans executed him for that crime under the charge 'king of the Jews'.

An unexpected Messiah

As shown earlier, the expected Messiah was viewed as a military leader who would expel the Roman occupying forces, extend the borders of the holy land and impose the law upon the covenantal people. The people took the promise of a new David literally, as one who would repeat the triumphs of the original David.

This explains why Jesus did not want it known in public that he was the Christ, except in Jerusalem at the end when he provided opportunity for the people to recognize their king. Had he done so earlier it would have created a furore and brought his ministry to a premature end. Thus, apart from his messianic admission to people in the temple courts and to the high priest (Mark 12:35–37; 14:61–62), Jesus sought to commend his messiahship wordlessly, by the quality of his life and by symbolic acts like riding up to the holy city and his clearing of the vendors from the temple. Jesus was a real, but hitherto hidden, Messiah.

Furthermore, he fundamentally redefined messiahship in three ways that were unexpected at that time.

First, he referred to himself as 'son of man'. In the Aramaic language of that day these words meant only 'a man' and could have been used as a roundabout way of saying 'I', so that when people heard Jesus speak like that it did not create any wild messianic rumours.

On the other hand, however, it is more probable that Jesus was echoing the prophet Daniel's dream vision of 'one like a son of man' who would come triumphantly to the ancient of days, God (Dan. 7:13–15). This 'Son of Man' is the most exalted figure we meet in the Old Testament. After the eventual fall of all the nations at the end of history, this 'one like a son of man' will rule over all peoples, from the presence of God. Daniel prophesied that 'all peoples, nations, and languages' would 'serve him' (Dan. 7:14).

However, the invariable presence of the article *the* in Jesus' references pointedly elevates Daniel's 'one *like* a son of man' into a title, '*the* Son of Man'. Moreover, as we review the occasions when Mark records Jesus using this terminology, we are struck by the way Jesus consistently sees his destiny in terms of Daniel's vision of a heavenly king. Jesus believes he is destined to be the ruler of the world. He uses the term 'the Son of Man' (never his disciples), and does so with remarkable concentration after Caesarea Philippi, when he begins his final journey to Jerusalem. For Jesus, then, his messiahship was ultimately heavenly and cosmic, applicable to all people, something that helps us understand why he came to be worshipped post-crucifixion.

Secondly, this Messiah who was *the* Son of Man was, even more profoundly, *the Son of God* his Father. Easy to miss are Jesus' words at Caesarea Philippi where the Son of Man refers to God as '*his* Father' (Mark 8:38). In other words, the Christ who is the Son of Man is the *filial* Son of God 'his Father', whom Daniel calls 'the ancient of days'. Jesus' words reveal the hitherto hidden character of Israel's God as the *Father* of the Christ, his Son. This is clear also from Matthew's account of the Caesarea Philippi incident, where Peter's confession of Jesus as the Christ has the additional words 'the Son of the living God' and where Jesus also speaks about God as 'my Father' (Matt. 16:13–20).

This, too, becomes a recurring theme from Caesarea Philippi onwards. Jesus teaches the chief priests in Jerusalem that, like the prophets, he was 'sent' from God, but in distinction from them is 'a *beloved* Son', who in God's sight is '*my* Son' (Mark 12:1–6). On the Mount of Olives Jesus calls himself '*the* Son' and refers to God as '*the* Father' (Mark 13:32), where the repeated definite article points to a unique relationship between the Son and the Father. In Gethsemane he prays as a Son to God with intimacy and confidence as '*Abba*, Father' (Mark 14:36). The Christ, who is to be the heavenly Son of Man, is the *filial* and *only* Son of God.

Equally striking, thirdly, is that Jesus is a vicariously *suffering* Messiah. At Caesarea Philippi Jesus began to lead his twelve disciples to the city of David, Jerusalem. That city, however, was controlled by the dynasty of Annas, whose sons and son-in-law, Caiaphas, held not only the supreme office of high priest in succession but the major subsidiary positions in the temple hierarchy as well. This family were known to be exploitative and brutal in their hold over the ordinary folk in the holy city, including the many hundreds of poorer priests who left their peasant work twice a year for rostered duties in the temple. They were hated for their nepotism and croneyism. Furthermore, like the other members of the small cohort of wealthy and powerful families in Judea, the Annas dynasty was compromised by their affiliation with the Roman authorities, upon whom they depended for their lucrative appointment.

Jesus the Messiah would come to Jerusalem to gather the 'lost sheep of the house of Israel' (Matt. 10:6; 15:24; Ezek. 34:23). He knew, though, that Israel would not acknowledge her long-awaited Messiah, even though he gave her this one last chance to do so (Luke 13:34–35; 19:41–44). In the depths of his understanding Jesus knew that the tenants of God's vineyard would reject the *beloved Son* of the owner so that the vineyard would inevitably be handed over to the peoples of the nations (Mark 12:7–11).

Thus, during that long trek south from Caesarea Philippi to the City of David, Jesus predicted his death on three occasions (Mark 8:31–32; 9:31; 10:32–34). It was no mere cleverly human prediction, however; his sufferings were divinely mandated. He *must* suffer (Mark 8:31), he said, where the word 'must' implies that those sufferings were the will of God his Father.

On one memorable occasion he explained *why* he had to suffer: 'For the Son of Man also came not to be served but to serve, and to give his life a ransom *for many*' (Mark 10:45).

Jesus, the Son of Man, came to be a servant, that is, to give his life to set *many* people free. Here Jesus is deliberately applying a prophecy of Isaiah to himself. This is the prophecy about the vicariously suffering Servant of the Lord:

> the righteous one, my servant
> [shall] make many . . . righteous;
> and he shall bear their iniquities . . .
> and made intercession for the transgressors
> (Isa. 53:11b–12)

The remarkable thing here is that Isaiah's *many* included the hated Gentile nations of the world (Isa. 52:15). Jesus said the same thing at the Last Supper in his words spoken over the cup of wine, 'This is my blood of the covenant, which is poured out for *many*' (Mark 14:24).

What does Jesus mean in saying that his death will be a ransom to liberate *many*? In a remarkable and brief parable Jesus speaks of Satan as a 'strong man' who keeps prisoners in a dungeon (Mark 3:27). But Jesus is the *stronger* man who will overpower Satan and set his prisoners free. This he did when he gave his life for others, including the peoples of the nations. In other words, the peoples of the world the Son of Man will come to rule he will first liberate from the dungeon of the strong man, Satan. He will do this by dying for them in Jerusalem, in obedience to the Father's will.

It will be clear by now that Jesus accepted Cephas' recognition of him as the Messiah but that he radically redefined that role as *eternal* (2 Sam. 7), as the filial *Son* of *Abba*, his Father (Isa. 7, 9, 11), and as vicarious *sufferer* for many (Isa. 52 – 53) (see pp. 133–135). He was not at all the militaristic Messiah of current Jewish expectation, but someone far greater. This radically different Messiah informed the understanding of those original disciples, who, although Jews, created a new kind of Judaism, a messianic Judaism for all people. This messianic Judaism is the subject of the body of texts we have come to call the 'New Testament'.

This prompts the question 'Who was responsible for this ingenious, altogether new thing?' The answer that many have given is that Paul was the (evil) genius who created this utterly unexpected Messiah. That answer, however, is certainly wrong. Paul did not write the Gospels, where Jesus reveals his mind by his words, nor was Paul's greatness shown by that kind of theological creativity. Rather, Paul's God-given brilliance was as applier of the *already-formed* messianism he received from the original disciples, which he adapted for the benefit of the Gentiles. The real genius of this new messianism was Jesus himself (if genius is the right word). Jesus did something that others had not done: evidently he searched the Scriptures to find the mind of God in detail for the role of Messiah that he sensed he had had from boyhood (Luke 2:49), and that was revealed to him objectively in the Jordan River by the voice of God: 'you are my beloved Son' (Mark 1:11; my tr.). In the years between boyhood and baptism I conclude that Jesus had scrutinized the sacred writings in preparation for the role he was to adopt from the time of his baptism.

All of this, however, forces us to ask about the historical basis of the Gospel of Mark. Is he just spinning a story, a clever piece of theological fiction?

Mark and history

In the early part of the second century Papias, Bishop of Hierapolis (Pamukkale in modern Turkey), provided an account of the origins of Mark's Gospel:

> And the Elder [John] was saying this: Mark, having become Peter's interpreter wrote accurately but not in order as many things as he *remembered* of the things said and done by the Lord.
>
> For Mark neither heard the Lord nor did he follow him, but later, as I said, he followed Peter.
>
> Peter arranged his teachings as anecdotes as need arose, although not as a collection of the Lord's teachings.
>
> So Mark did nothing wrong in writing some things as he *remembered*

them. His single intention was not to omit anything he had heard nor to falsify anything in them. (Eusebius, *History of the Church* 3.39.15, quoting Irenaeus)[5]

It is usually assumed that Papias wrote circa 130, though some argue for a date as early as circa 110. Whatever the date, Papias depended for his information about Mark's Gospel on John the Elder who depended for his information on 'the disciples of the Lord'. The point is that the Elder John's report to Papias came from 'disciples of the Lord'; that is, in the first century, perhaps as early as circa 80. See below.

70(?)	80	110(?)
Mark wrote Gospel	Disciples of the Lord	Elder told Papias
	told Elder	

There is no way we can be sure about the precise dates. For example, Mark may have written his Gospel some years earlier than 70 and the Elder may have spoken to Papias some years later than 110. The important thing, however, is not the exactness of the years but the principle of the correct transmission of knowledge about the origin of Mark's Gospel.

There is an important thing to note here: Papias has some negative things to say about the Gospel of Mark, signalled by his words 'So Mark did nothing wrong'. Which 'wrongs' might Mark have committed? Primarily, he was not an immediate follower of the Lord and committed Peter's oral instructions to paper only at a later date, based on his memory. Papias appears to have viewed Mark's Gospel as inferior to the Gospel written by John, who *was* an associate of the Lord and who wrote his Gospel based on *his own* direct memory of the words and deeds of the Lord. Further, Mark did not write his Gospel 'in order', which implies its inferiority to Luke, who wrote an '*orderly* account' (Luke 1:3). In other words, Papias is not revealing a pro-Markan bias, but on the contrary gives only a qualified endorsement. Papias' mention of Mark's shortcomings helps us to accept the strengths of this Gospel that were not apparent to Papias or his contemporaries but are seen as invaluable today.

And great strengths these are. In fact, Papias' information about Mark's Gospel resolves the most pressing question of all. That is, Papias tells us once and for all how the things the Lord said and did came to be written, to provide access to the historical Messiah by those of us who were not Jesus' original disciples.

Our clue here is the twofold reference to Mark's 'memory': he 'wrote accurately . . . as many things as he *remembered*' and 'Mark . . . writing some things as he *remembered* them'. Some scholars believe (wrongly, in my opinion) that the words and works of Christ were relayed by generations of village storytellers (and inevitably corrupted in the process) before being blindly recorded by Mark. On the contrary, the Elder John related what really happened. What the Lord said and did was taught by the pre-eminent eyewitness Peter, and recorded by his 'interpreter' Mark, based on Mark's recollection of Peter's words that he had heard and (verbally) translated many times.

In other words, they are wrong who assert that generations of faceless raconteurs were interposed between Jesus and our earliest written Gospel text. Between Christ and that written text stand only two persons, persons whose *names are known to us*: Peter the teacher and Mark his interpreter and scribe. It is unclear from Papias when Mark wrote down Peter's words: soon afterwards, or at/after Peter's passing. In the end, *when* this was written matters less than knowing *who* it was that wrote. The *who* in question was Mark, an accomplished and well-connected leader throughout the generation following the lifespan of the historical Messiah.[6]

If Papias' information is correct, we would expect to find traces of Peter's influence in this Gospel, and that is precisely what we find.

The dominant role of Peter

Upon examination we discover that Peter enjoys a special role within Mark's Gospel.[7]

The *first* disciple Mark has Jesus meet is Peter (1:16; he is called Simon until 3:16), and the *last* disciple we hear of is Peter (16:7). The references to Peter at the beginning and the end are striking and create a 'frame' around the whole Gospel.[8] Richard Bauckham notes that 'according to literary convention of the time the most authoritative eyewitness is the one who was present at the events from their beginning to their end and who can therefore vouch for the overall shape of the story as well as for specific key events'.[9] According to that convention, Mark identifies Peter as the key witness for his narrative.

Consistent with Peter as the main witness we also find that Mark has Peter present throughout the greater part of his narrative. Peter's name (as 'Peter' or 'Simon') occurs remarkably often in Mark: no fewer than twenty-six times. After Peter, the Zebedee brothers James and John appear next most frequently: nine times in all. Yet in all but two cases they are mentioned with Peter. Apart from the list of the Twelve (3:16–19), the only other disciples Mark mentions are Peter's brother Andrew (three times) and Judas Iscariot (once). So Peter is a dominating presence as the prime eyewitness in Mark's Gospel, though his shortcomings are not glossed over (8:32; 14:29–72). This observation provides powerful support for the testimony of the Elder John to Papias that Peter was the eyewitness source for the Gospel Mark wrote.

There are numerous details in Mark's Gospel that support the Elder's report to Papias that an eyewitness (Peter) is the source of this Gospel.

Chronologically connected blocks

Although much of Mark is not tightly sequential, there are a number of chronologically connected blocks; for example, Jesus' first day in *Capernaum* (1:21–32), his teaching at the *lakeside* followed by his *crossing* of the lake (4:1 – 5:21), the later *recrossing* of the lake (6:30–53), the *journey* from Caesarea Philippi to the high mountain, after six days (8:27 – 9:2).

It could be claimed that Mark has invented 'facts' to create the impression of a truthful narrative. But why would he do this in these few instances rather than in the whole narrative? It is more probable that Mark has specifically remembered these sequences from Peter's narration of them and that the more vague sequences are due to the limitations of Mark's memory.

Nazareth and Capernaum

Mark's references to Capernaum and Nazareth are sufficiently coherent to answer the claim that his Gospel is a haphazard collection of episodes.

The 'house' in Capernaum was home to Simon and Andrew and their direct and extended families. It was to this 'house' in Capernaum that Jesus came, where he initially stayed and to which he returned after various journeys elsewhere. These Capernaum 'house' references span the various episodes throughout the Galilee chapters (Mark 1:29; 1:33, 35–36; 2:1; 3:19; [7:17]; 9:33).

According to Mark, Jesus left Nazareth to be baptized by John in the Jordan, but later came to Capernaum (Mark 1:29; cf. Matt. 4:13). Jesus is routinely called 'Jesus of Nazareth' or 'the Nazarene, Jesus' (Mark 1:24; 10:47; 16:6; 14:67). When he returned at last to Nazareth, the people were so sceptical that it provoked his famous aphorism 'a prophet is not without honour, except in his own country' (Mark 6:4). Those who did not honour this prophet were 'those of his own country' (district), 'his own kin' (extended family) and 'his own house' (immediate family including mother, brothers and sisters; Mark 6:3; my tr.).

This scepticism in Nazareth was not new. Earlier his 'family', that is, his mother and brothers, had set out from Nazareth to Capernaum to 'seize' him. On arrival they were 'outside' (the house?) whereupon Jesus commented that his true mother and father were those who did the will of God (Mark 3:21–35).

This linkage between these two villages spans four chapters and consistently points up the unbelief of his biological family in contrast with the welcome of the new 'family' in Capernaum.

This Capernaum–Nazareth distinction is not a major theme in Mark. It does, nonetheless, in a quiet way support the idea of Mark's dependence on a reliable witness, who saw things from a Capernaum viewpoint.

Evasive withdrawals

One of the features of the early chapters is that Jesus frequently withdraws from situations and people. These evasive movements are listed in Harold Hoehner's biography of Herod Antipas, where Hoehner observes that frequently these withdrawals make 'good historical sense'.[10]

Mark's narrative is characterized by the often-bewildering references to Jesus' movements. Sometimes these involve crossings of the lake and sometimes across the borders into Tyre or Sidon or into Philip's tetrarchy or to the Decapolis. It is not always possible to account for the reason or the route taken. Yet the movements are able to be explained in part by the nature of Jesus' ministry, which, on one hand, provoked crowd interest in his healings, and, on the other, the hostility of the Pharisees and more particularly of the tetrarch and his faction (the 'Herodians').[11] Once more, the appearance of these details is consistent with Mark's recollection of Peter's teachings.

Vivid details

There are examples of vivid detail in the Gospel of Mark, but where do they come from? If they were present in all the stories in the Galilee, we might be inclined to view them as contrived. Their haphazard occurrences, however, in which they are confined to small details, tend to support their authenticity. Here are five examples.

1:32–33:

> That evening, at sundown, they were bringing to him all who were sick or possessed with demons. And the whole city was gathered together about [*pros*] the door.

The sabbath has passed and the incapacitated can now be brought to him; the whole village has gathered, expectantly facing the door of the house. This dramatic scene is beyond literary invention.

4:36–38:

> And leaving the crowd, they took him with them in the boat, just as he was. And other boats were with him. And a great storm of wind arose, and the waves beat into the boat, so that the boat was already filling. But he was in the stern, asleep on the cushion . . .

The details 'just as he was', the 'other boats' and Jesus 'asleep on a cushion' are at the same time so vivid and gratuitous as to question a fiction-based imagination as to the sources.

5:2–5:

> there met him out of the tombs a man with an unclean spirit, who lived among the tombs; and no one could bind him any more, even with a chain; for he had often been bound with fetters and chains, but the chains he wrenched apart, and the fetters he broke in pieces; and no one had the strength to subdue him. Night and day among the tombs and on the mountains he was always crying out, and bruising himself with stones.

Mark's images of this disturbed man who was prodigiously strong, with broken chains hanging from wrists and ankles, are potent and, again, credibly written from an eyewitness's recollection.

5:38–41:

> When they came to the house of the ruler of the synagogue, he saw a tumult, and people weeping and wailing loudly. And when he had entered, he said to them, 'Why do you make a tumult and weep? The child is not dead but sleeping.' And they laughed at him. But he put them all outside, and took the child's father and mother and those who were with him, and went in where the child was. Taking her by the hand he said to her, 'Talitha cumi'; which means, 'Little girl, I say to you, arise.'

The name of the synagogue leader, Jairus, the sounds of wailing, the laughter and the Aramaic words all contribute to a strong sense of an eyewitness account.

6:39–40:

> Then he commanded them all to sit down by companies upon the green grass. So they sat down in groups [literally, 'garden beds'], by hundreds and by fifties.

This is an almost photographic image of people seated in ordered groups, their colourful gowns giving the appearance of garden beds set in green grass.

The words from these passages in Mark's Gospel leap from the page. Most probably they spring from the memory of someone who was struck by the scene or the drama of the moment or the impact of the sounds. If such details were constant throughout, we could perhaps explain them as literary invention. Their occasional appearance, however, speaks against that explanation. A storyteller who was an eyewitness is the most probable reason for the appearance of these striking details.

Jesus' emotions

Prominent among the vivid details in Mark's Gospel are Jesus' emotional responses in various situations. These are some examples.

1:40–43:

And a leper came to him beseeching him, and kneeling said to him . . . Moved with pity, [12] he . . . touched him . . . . And he *sternly charged him, and sent him* away at once . . .

3:1, 2, 5:

Again he entered the synagogue, and a man was there who had a withered hand. And they watched him, to see whether he would heal him on the Sabbath, so that they might accuse him . . . . And he looked around at them *with anger, grieved* at their hardness of heart . . .

6:34:

As he went ashore he saw a great throng, and he had *compassion* on them, because they were like sheep without a shepherd . . .

10:13–14:

And they were bringing children to him, that he might touch them; and the disciples rebuked them. But when Jesus saw it he was *indignant*, and said to them, 'Let the children come to me, do not hinder them; for to such belongs the kingdom of God . . .'

14:33–34:

And he took with him Peter and James and John, and began to be greatly *distressed* and *troubled*. And he said to them, 'My soul is very sorrowful, even to death . . .

Are these observations of Jesus' emotions the result of Mark's literary creativity or of his recollection of Peter's words? If the former, we would expect a more systematic development of these emotions. The writer's passing mention of them points rather in the direction of his recall of Peter's own reactions to Jesus in these situations.

Furthermore, on five occasions Mark observes that Jesus 'looked around', as in a circle (Greek, *periblepomai*):

3:5 – in the synagogue when they watched if he would heal on the sabbath
3:34 – in the house in Capernaum, with mother and brothers outside
5:32 – at the crowd to see who touched him
10:23 – to the disciples when he said how hard it was for the wealthy to enter the kingdom of God
11:11 – on his arrival in the temple

Each of these was a dramatic occasion and Jesus' circular manner of 'looking around' left its imprint on Peter's memory. Matthew does not use this word and Luke does so only once (6:10).

Summary

The prominent place of Peter in the Gospel of Mark is a striking confirmation of the Elder's assertion that Peter was the source of Mark's Gospel, based on Mark's memory of Peter's teachings. The inexact sequence of the Gospel at some points supports the Elder John's comment that Mark did not write in precise sequence. That said, however, Mark's Gospel overall is probably a fair overall representation of the events as they occurred. There is circumstantial evidence in the small number of specifically connected sequences, the subtle interplay between two villages (Nazareth and Capernaum), Jesus' various withdrawals and the small details, including those related to emotions that, considered cumulatively, support the primary role of Peter as the source of information in the Gospel of Mark.

Messiah in Mark

There is ample evidence from those times that the Jews were expecting the Messiah, the descendant of David, and even stronger evidence from the Gospel of Mark that Peter and the disciples came to recognize Jesus as that Messiah and that Jesus believed himself to be that Messiah. It is firmly historical that the Romans crucified Jesus at the request of the temple leaders for presenting himself as the Messiah; that is, as 'king of the Jews'.

Jesus, however, was to the Jews of that time an unrecognizable Messiah. He saw himself as the Son of Man (destined to rule the universe), as Son of God his Father, but as the vicarious substitute in his death for the liberation of many from the nations.

It is difficult to escape the proposition that Jesus himself reshaped the idea of Messiah, based on his sense of sonship of God, informed by his own deep study of the sacred writings and objectively confirmed by the audible voice of God at his baptism in the Jordan River.

Finally, there is strong evidence that Mark's Gospel was written out of the author's recollection of Peter's eyewitness-based preaching.

6. MESSIAH'S BIRTH

For centuries, Jewish hopes for deliverance had focused on the Messiah, a descendant of king David, according to the promises of the Lord mediated through his prophets (see earlier, pp. 21–38). The conviction of the New Testament was that he belonged to the line of David and was the predestined Messiah.

David and Jesus

The two earliest creeds of Christianity were formulated in Jerusalem soon after Jesus' historical lifespan. Both assert that he was the Messiah:

[God's] Son, who was descended from *David* . . .

Christ died for our sins . . . was buried . . . was raised [resurrected] . . . appeared to . . . (Rom. 1:3; 1 Cor. 15:3; cf. 2 Tim. 2:8)

Given the earliness of these statements, we logically conclude that Jesus' identity as Messiah was established in the minds of his disciples before his death, and that they had been formulated after the first Easter in the terms Paul 'received'. Since the disciples believed Jesus was the Christ, we reasonably conclude that Jesus himself believed he was the Christ. In turn, this implies that his parents Joseph and Mary knew that their son belonged to the line of David. Two pieces of evidence support this view.

First, in their genealogies Matthew and Luke indicate that Joseph was descended from David (Matt. 1:6, 16; Luke 3:23, 31). This is probably historically correct and not merely, as it were, a theological gloss. Matthew and Luke diverge so completely in their genealogies in most other elements in their lists of names that their *common* assertion of Joseph as descendant of David is enhanced.[1] Collusion would have issued in detailed agreement, not detailed disagreement! In the genealogies of Matthew and Luke we have two discrete sources, not one derived from the other or two dependent upon an earlier common source.

Secondly, the Flavian emperors of Rome (69–96), who had led the Romans against the Jews in the war (66–70), were understandably nervous about Jewish messianic movements and potential uprisings throughout the empire. A Jewish messiah would have been seen as a political threat to their imperial dynasty, in particular a descendant of the line of David (Eusebius, *History of the Church* 3.12). Accordingly, Emperor Domitian (81–96) ordered the execution of all who were descended from David (Eusebius, *History of the Church* 3.12). Among those under suspicion were the grandsons of Jude, brother of Jesus, who were brought (from Galilee?) to Rome to stand before Domitian. When the emperor saw the calluses on the hands of these peasants and learned of the smallness of their land holding, he sent them home: they were not potential messiahs posing a threat to his empire. Jude's grandsons did not dispute their Davidic origin. Clearly, their great-grandfather Joseph was from the line of David.

In short, Jesus of Nazareth was a 'son' of Joseph, descended from king David.

Nazareth

Nazareth was a tiny, obscure village, finding no reference in the Old Testament, in the writings of Josephus or in the Talmud. It is mentioned only in the Gospels and the book of Acts. However, in 1962 the place name 'Netzer' was discovered on an inscription in a synagogue in Caesarea Maritima.[2] It was a place to which the priestly Elkalir family would migrate after the destruction of Jerusalem in AD 135.

Archaeological investigation of Nazareth suggests it was uninhabited from the eighth to the second centuries BC. There is an absence of ceramic remains from the Assyrian, Persian and early Hellenistic periods.[3] This is consistent with two known events. One is the invasion by the Assyrian Tiglath-Pileser in 733 BC, when the people of Galilee were taken into captivity to Assyria, after which Galilee became a Gentile region. Isaiah the prophet reflects this crisis: 'In the former time he brought into contempt the land of Zebulun and the land of Naphtali.' Yet, Isaiah promised, '[God] . . . will make glorious . . . Galilee of the nations. The people who walked in darkness have seen a great light' (Isa. 9:1–2).

This unoccupied circumstance changed with a second known event. During the rule of the Maccabean king John Hyrcanus (134–104 BC), the Jews reconquered Galilee. In the years following, many Jews settled in Galilee, including, I suggest, the Davidic forebears of Joseph. We do not know where they may have come from in migrating to Nazareth. Perhaps they came from the Jewish dispersion in Mesopotamia, descendants of exiles from earlier deportations. Whatever the case, by Jesus' time the small village of Nazareth was, to a significant degree, probably composed of a Davidic clan. Jesus, along with most of the inhabitants of Nazareth, belonged to the same extended family, descended from David, the king of Israel.

This may explain the much-discussed statement of Matthew: '[Jesus] went and dwelt in a city called Nazareth, that what was spoken by the prophets might be fulfilled, "He shall be called a Nazarene [*Nazōraios*]"' (Matt. 2:23). But there is no such oracle to be found in the writings of the prophets. However, attention has been drawn to Isaiah 11:1, 'a branch [Hebrew, *neṣer*] shall grow from its roots'.

Is Matthew's appeal to 'the prophets' a broad reference to the many Old Testament promises for a descendant of David to come to Israel, but with a particular play on the word *neṣer*, 'branch', from Isaiah 11:1, Jeremiah 23:5 and Zechariah 3:8, 6:12–13?[4] Though the royal line was hacked down to a stump, from that stump a root or branch would spring up. Matthew may be saying of Jesus, 'He shall be called that "branch" of David,' that is, his long awaited 'son', the Messiah of Israel. The writer of the Apocalypse, too, is aware of Jesus as the 'branch' of David in the words 'I am the *root* and the offspring of David . . .' (Rev. 22:16; cf. 5:5).

This understanding is entirely in line with Matthew's opening words 'The book of the genealogy of Jesus Christ, the son of David . . .' and with the entire Davidic tenor of the genealogy (see Matt. 1:5–6, 17). The genealogy is followed by the words of an angel addressed to 'Joseph, *son of David* . . .' (Matt. 1:20). Matthew's account, which immediately moves to the birth of Jesus in *Bethlehem*, David's birthplace, could not be more pointed. In Matthew's mind Jesus is the royal son of David, born in Bethlehem, David's ancestral home.

We may surmise that the long-uninhabited village of Nazareth came to take its name from the Davidides who settled there during the Maccabaean era in the second century BC. The similarity between *neṣer* and 'Nazareth' is apparent.[5] It was quite common for places to take their names from the tribe or clan who settled there; for example, Danites from Dan to the north of the Sea of Galilee. An association between Nazareth, the home of a *Nazarēnos* (a descendant of David), may be discerned in the words of Bartimaeus, the blind beggar from Jericho. When he heard that it was Jesus the *Nazarēnos* who was passing by, he cried out, 'Jesus, *son of David* have mercy on me' (Mark 10:47).

As noted above, the grandsons of Jude were brought before Domitian. According to Eusebius, who quotes Hegesippus, an earlier authority, these men testified that Jesus was the Messiah (whose kingdom was heavenly, not political). Since, as seems probable, Nazareth was a Davidic village where Jesus' extended family lived, Jude's grandsons may have come from that same place. The book of Acts speaks of the spread of Christianity in Galilee (Acts 9:31), where it is probable that the relatives of Jesus, though dismissive of his messianic claims during his ministry (John 7:5), became leaders in the nascent church of Galilee.

Mary

Little is known of the background of Mary (Mariam). None of the biblical sources supplies the names of her parents,[6] nor of the tribe to which she belonged. Her kinswoman Elizabeth was descended from Aaron the priest (Luke 1:5, 36). Was Mary also of priestly descent? This is improbable, since Jesus was not from the priestly tribe of Aaron but from the tribe of Judah (to which David belonged; Heb. 7:14). Jewish ethnicity and tribal descent were reckoned as through the mother. So Mary as well as Joseph probably belonged to the same tribe, Judah. Mary, like Joseph, lived in Nazareth in Galilee (Luke 1:26–27),[7] which as I have suggested was a Davidic settlement.

According to custom, Mary's father had betrothed her for a marriage, probably in her middle or late teens (Matt. 1:18). The Gospels describe her as a young woman (Greek, *parthenos*; Luke 1:27), which in that society meant a virgin.

The few references to Mary during Jesus' public ministry suggest she was a woman of some standing and prominence within her own small world. At the marriage at Cana, a neighbouring village to the north of Nazareth, Mary 'was there', whereas Jesus was '*also* invited'; Mary took charge when the wine failed (John 2:1, 3, 6). Her day's journey from Nazareth to lakeside Capernaum to retrieve Jesus from the house of Peter when she saw him to be 'beside himself' is further indication of her determination (Mark 3:21–31).

Born of a virgin

According to Matthew and Luke, Mary conceived her son Jesus independently of a man: Joseph was not the biological father of Jesus. This virginal conception is without precedent in the Old Testament and without real parallel in Graeco-Roman writers.

True, there are some parallels in, for example, the birth of Samson, but this probably occurred by natural procreative process (Judg. 13:2–24; cf. Luke 1:5–7). In the Gentile world notable men like Plato, Pythagoras, Alexander the Great and the emperor Augustus were said to have been born of the union of their respective mothers and various gods. However, these stories are told in improbable ways. Snakes were involved in the impregnation of the mothers of Alexander and Augustus. It is doubtful that the writers intended their accounts to be taken literally: they were myths to convey the special qualities of the people in question. A Gentile convert like Ignatius (late first century), who would have been well versed in mythological writings, is in no doubt about Jesus' birth. Writing to the Christians in Smyrna early in the second century, Ignatius observes:

> you are established in immoveable faith . . . being fully persuaded as
> touching our Lord that he is in truth of the family of David according
> to the flesh, God's son by the will and power of God,
> truly born of a virgin . . . (*Smyrnaeans* 1.1–2)[8]

The narratives of both Matthew and Luke, though told from different perspectives, establish that the child Jesus was conceived by the Holy Spirit independently of the biological procreative process (Matt. 1:18; Luke 1:27, 34–35).[9] Each genealogy also establishes in its own way that Joseph was not the biological father. In Matthew's genealogy each man listed was the 'father' of x, who was to be the 'father' of y, and so on. But with Joseph the pattern is broken. Joseph is not the 'father of Jesus' but rather, and pointedly, 'Joseph [was] the *husband* of Mary, of whom Jesus was born' (Matt. 1:16; cf. Mark 6:3). In Luke's genealogy each man listed is the 'son' of x who is the 'son' of y, in reverse order back to Adam. But in the case of Jesus, the first name listed, Luke writes, 'Jesus . . . being the son (*as was supposed*) of Joseph' (Luke 3:23). Thus both genealogies in distinctive ways establish that Joseph was not the biological father of Jesus.

It is often commented that the rest of the New Testament is silent about the virgin conception. It is true that, with one exception, the letters do not mention the circumstances of Jesus' birth. But then they say little about his historical life or ministry. These letters make no mention of Mary or Joseph, nor, for that matter do they speak of Jesus as a teacher or worker of miracles.

This should not surprise us, because the letters were not the initial communication to the churches, which was by word of mouth. The letters are follow-up documents written not for evangelistic but for pastoral purposes, for the benefit of those who had already become Christians. Those who first heard about Jesus would have wanted to know who he was and the circumstances of his birth and upbringing. In response, those who first brought the message would have told their hearers various biographical details about Jesus. It is difficult to believe that they would not have told the hearers about his parents, early life and ministry.

Such initial oral teaching was later supplemented by written texts narrating phases of Jesus' ministry and teachings. These were committed early to written form and circulated to many of the churches (see Luke 1:1–2). Probably, accounts of Jesus' birth were among these, and Matthew's and Luke's versions grew out of such sources.

Only one allusion to the virgin birth is found outside the Gospels – in Paul's letter to the Galatian churches:

> When the time had fully come
> God sent forth his Son,
> born of a woman,
> born under the law,
> to redeem those who were under the law . . .
> (Gal. 4:4)

The solemn cadence of these words suggests they were a creed or confession, not merely written *de novo* by Paul, nor heard for the first time by the Galatians. Indeed, they appear to summarize sections of Luke's narrative.

1. Luke's '[God] has visited and *redeemed* his people . . . as he spoke by the mouths of his holy prophets' (Luke 1:68–70) is summed up in Paul's words above, 'The time had fully come . . . to *redeem*'.

2. Luke's 'He . . . will be called *Son* of the Most High' (Luke 1:32) is closely related to Paul's 'God sent forth his *Son*'.[10]

3. Luke's account of the angel's announcement to Mary of the supernatural conception of a son and his comment in the genealogy ('Jesus . . . being the son (*as was supposed*) of Joseph' (Luke 3:23.) are neatly captured by Paul's words that Jesus was: 'born of a *woman*'.

4. Luke's account of the parents' presentation of the child in the temple and, later, their annual visit to Jerusalem for the Passover (which included the youthful Jesus' first Passover visit to Jerusalem) 'according to the custom of the *law*' (Luke 2:27, 41) is encapsulated in Paul's observation that Jesus was 'born under the *law*'.

In the light of these similarities of concept, though not of exact wording, it seems probable that Paul knew of the underlying tradition about Jesus' birth that would find more complete form in the early chapters of the Gospel of Luke. Historically, Paul's brief summary in a letter written in all probability before AD 50 is an early witness to the circumstances of the birth of Jesus.

Matthew, having indicated in his genealogy that Jesus was 'born . . . of Mary' and that Joseph was 'husband of Mary' (but not father of Jesus), said this fulfilled Isaiah's prophecy:

> Behold, a virgin shall conceive and bear a son,
> and his name shall be called Emmanuel.
> (Matt. 1:23; Isa. 7:14)

The virgin conception and Davidic descent

The genealogies of Matthew and Luke both establish Jesus' descent from David, through Joseph. But the virginal conception of the child through Mary indicates that Joseph was not the biological father. Does this break the physical connection between

David and Jesus and call into question his eligibility to be known as the Messiah of Israel?

Two factors bear on this. One is that Mary may have been herself, like Joseph, of the line of David. As noted above, she was most probably from the tribe of Judah and her home was Nazareth, a probable Davidic clan settlement. The likelihood is that all the inhabitants were of the same tribe, in which case she, too, was of Davidic descent, betrothed to a man from her own tribe.

The other is that, in any case, Joseph acted as the legal father in the naming and registering of his son (Matt. 1:20–21; Luke 2:1–5). Under levirate marriage the son was *legally* regarded as the son of the deceased man (Deut. 25:5–10). Since biological and legal paternity were not identical, it was possible for Joseph to be regarded as the legal father although he was not the biological father. Certainly, Jesus was known as the 'son of Joseph' (John 1:45; cf. 6:42, as noted above). In other words, based on Isaiah's prophecy, now fulfilled, Jesus is the Christ and Immanuel, God with us. Matthew wants us to understand the *deity* of the Messiah. Later, Peter will address Jesus as 'the Christ, the Son of the living God' (Matt. 16:16).

Joseph and Mary's descent from David qualified Jesus as the Messiah, but the virginal conception by Mary established his deity.

Conclusion

All the evidence points to Jesus belonging to the line of David, which potentially qualified him to be the Messiah. This did not automatically make Jesus the Christ, since there must have been other descendants of David alive in Jesus' day. God singled Jesus out to be the Messiah, and this was revealed to him by his study of the Holy Scriptures and confirmed by the voice of God at his baptism in the Jordan and further confirmed to his disciples by his miracles, as foreshadowed by the prophets (see below, pp. 136–137).

7. MESSIAH'S MESSAGE

It must be regarded as historically secure that Jesus taught the people of Israel by parables. The statistics are impressive. Mark records *eleven* parables (nine are repeated in Matthew and Luke), *nine* are common to Matthew and Luke (the Q source), *ten* are peculiar to Matthew (the M source), and *fifteen* are found only in Luke (the L source). When to these forty-five parables we add the allegories of the good shepherd and the true vine from the Gospel of John, it becomes evident that parable teaching was fundamental to the activities of Jesus of Nazareth. The appearance of parables in originally discrete, independent sources is strong evidence that Jesus taught in parables.

Doubtless Jesus spoke many more parables than those that have survived in the Gospels. Mark comments that Jesus did not speak to the crowds 'without a parable', but explained their meaning to his immediate disciples in private (Mark 4:34).

Rabbis' parables

The centrality of parable teaching for Jesus is consistent with Jewish culture of that era. Mainstream rabbis also taught in parables (though, as we shall see, Jesus' parables were significantly different). Following is an example of a parable from Jesus' times. The speaker, Rabbi Eleazar, is comforting another rabbi, Johanan ben Zakkai, whose son has died:

> I will tell you a parable.
> How shall we liken the matter?
> To a man who received from a king an object for safe keeping.
> Overwhelmed by his sense of responsibility, he used to cry
>   every day.
> 'O, if only I could get quit of the worry of this trust!'
> Well, you likewise, master had a son;
> He made himself familiar with the law in all its branches;
> and then he departed this world without sin.
> Should you not then be amenable to comforting,
> Since you have fortunately restored to God what he entrusted
>   to you?[1]

The structure is simple: (1) a story, followed by (2) the application: 'Well, *you* [Johanan] likewise . . .' In the story, which is an allegory, 'the man' is Johanan, 'the king' is God and the object 'entrusted' is Johanan's dead son. The setting is one of domestic tragedy and the parable's intent is pastoral.

At least one of Jesus' parables also had a 'pastoral' setting, where Jesus was asked to adjudicate between two brothers over an inheritance dispute. In his parable of the rich fool, however, Jesus pointedly declined the request but instead told a story illustrating the folly of covetousness (Luke 12:13–21). In Eleazar's parable the death of Johanan's son was the *occasion* for the parable, whereas in his parable Jesus *introduced* the matter of death (of the rich fool). This betrays a consistent element in Jesus' parables: the urgency of time.

The Messiah and time

Jesus regarded himself as the centre point of salvation history.
Consider his first recorded words in Galilee following his baptism
in the Jordan: 'The *time* is fulfilled, and the kingdom of God is at
hand; repent, and believe in the gospel' (Mark 1:15; cf. Matt. 4:17).

This is a dramatic, highly charged statement. Jesus, having cast
his eye backwards over the two millennia of sacred writings,
declares that the 'time'[2] for their prophecies to be fulfilled has now
come. Then casting his eye forward, he says that the future
kingdom of God at the end of history has now begun, in his own
words and actions. On subway station platforms passengers feel
the rush of air from the tunnel before the incoming, but as yet
unseen, train arrives. Likewise, the future kingdom of God was
visibly and *audibly* present ahead of its advent in the deeds and
words of the Messiah Jesus.

How, then, are we to understand 'the kingdom of God'? The
sacred writings celebrated the kingdom of the Lord's anointed,
David, as the greatest moment in Israel's history. The Lord
promised to establish David's kingdom for ever (2 Sam. 7:13).
Despite David's commitment to the Lord, however, the human
king was deeply flawed (2 Sam. 7:18–29; 12:14).

The kingdom of 'great David's greater Son' would not be
a mere continuation of David's line of rulers. Rather, Jesus'
announcement of the kingdom *of God* pointed to a new, flawless
and absolutely final thing, never to be superseded or abrogated.
See the figure below.

Law and Prophets → **Messiah** ← kingdom of God

In other words, Jesus places himself and his words at the centre of
history. He speaks both retrospectively ('the time is fulfilled') and
prospectively ('the kingdom of God is at hand'). This oracle, given
at the commencement of his ministry in Galilee, marks the end of
the beginning of salvation history and the beginning of its end.

Secular historians are interested in world history, but the Bible
cares little about the history of what *humans* are doing. The Bible's
real interest is what *God* has done, is doing and will do. In the

perspective of the Bible, human history is thus a sideshow.[3] If this is true of the narratives of the books of the Old Testament, it is true to an infinitely greater degree of the words of the Messiah, Jesus. His mind was filled with *God's* narrative of salvation history in which he saw himself as the midpoint.

Kingdom parables

Are we able to organize these dozens of Jesus parables thematically? At first this seems a daunting task, since the stories and their settings are so complex. Upon further thought, however, there is a unifying theme: a time line. By this I mean a time line that traces the progress of the kingdom of God that (1) begins with Jesus, (2) continues with the behaviour of his followers, and (3) ends with the final revelation of the kingdom of God.

Initiation of the kingdom

When Jesus initially declared that the kingdom of God was at hand, he accompanied that announcement by a dramatic action, the casting out of unclean spirits (see e.g. Mark 1:21–28; 3:11; 5:1–20). This provoked fierce opposition from the scribes, who attributed Jesus' powers to Satan. Jesus responded to this criticism in his parable of the strong man, where he portrays himself as a stronger than Satan, at *first* binding this strong man (right now) but who will *then* (later) have his house plundered (Mark 3:23–27). In other words, the kingdom of God is active in Jesus' expulsion of unclean spirits in anticipation of the wholesale defeat of Satan at a later time (at the Messiah's death and resurrection). The parable has a time line that begins with Jesus' present activity (*first*) and ends at a climactic later point (*then*).

Jesus' kingdom preaching was accompanied by another provocative activity: his table fellowship with sinners (see p. 97). Like his expulsion of unclean spirits, this also attracted criticism from the scribes, and several of Jesus' parables were spoken in response. In the twin parables of the unshrunk cloth and the new wineskins, Jesus teaches that his kingdom message is radically new and not a mere 'patching up' of a corrupted old covenant (Mark 2:21–22).

Jesus' welcome of the sinners in table fellowship expressed the radical nature of divine grace in the kingdom of God. His parable of the labourers in the vineyard (Matt. 20:1–16) was his pointed adaptation of a current rabbinic parable that had taught something diametrically opposite: God rewards people according to their works:

> It is like a king who hired many labourers. But one was outstanding in his work. What did the king do? He took him away and walked to and fro with him. When it was evening, the labourers came to receive their pay, and he gave him, with them, the full amount of their wage. Then the labourers murmured and said, 'We have worked the whole day, and this man has worked only two hours.' Then the king said, 'This man has done more in two hours than you have done in the whole day.'[4]

In this parable the labourer who received a full day's pay for only two hours' work was rewarded for doing more than those who had laboured all day. Jesus, however, radically reworked the parable to teach that the kingdom is grounded in God's mercy rather than man's rights.

Rather than rewarding those who sought to approach God based on their works, Jesus taught that *God himself* takes the initiative in searching for 'sinners', those 'lost' from him. Luke records this unexpected reality in the parable of the lost sheep and its adjunct parables of the lost coin and the lost sons (Luke 15:8–10). The latter parables are also Jesus' adaptation of existing rabbinic parables that taught very differently.

In the parable of the lost coin Rabbi Phineas ben Jair urges his hearers to search for the Torah as one searches for hidden treasure:[5]

> A parable. It is like a man who if he loses a sela [half a shekel] or an obol in his house, he lights lamp after lamp, wick after wick, until he finds it.
>
> But behold, if for these things that are only ephemeral and of this world a man will light so many lamps and lights till he finds where they are hidden, how much more ought you search for the words of the

Torah, which are the life both of this world and the next world, as for
hidden treasure? Hence, 'If you seek her as silver . . . ' etc.
Note: the sela and the obol were valuable coins.

In Jesus' parable of the lost coin it is Jesus (representing his
Father) who, in eating with sinners, seeks the lost (Luke 15:1–2).
Jesus' implied rejection of the Torah as the appropriate object to
search for and his implicit identification of himself with God
searching for the lost was probably outrageous and offensive.

In his parable of the wayward son Rabbi Meir spoke about a
son of a king who followed evil ways but was too ashamed to
return to his father.[6] Rabbi Meir's parable is about the nation Israel
who are urged to return to their father, God:

> Unto what is the matter like? It is like a son of a king who took to evil
> ways.
>
> The king sent a tutor to him, saying: Repent my son. But the son sent
> him back to his father [with a message], How can I have the effrontery
> to return? I am ashamed to come before you. Thereupon the father sent
> back word: my son, is a son ever ashamed to return to his father? And
> is it not to your father that you will be returning?
>
> Even so the Holy One, blessed be He, sent Jeremiah to Israel when they
> sinned, and said to him: Go, say to my children: Return. Whence is this?
> For it is said: 'Go and proclaim these words' etc. (Jer 3:12). Israel asked
> Jeremiah: How can we have the effrontery to return to God? Whence do
> we know this? For it is said: 'Let us lie down in our shame and let our
> confusion cover us' etc. (v. 25). But God sent back word to them: My
> children, if you return, will you not be returning to your Father?
>
> Whence is this? 'For I am become a father to Israel' etc. (Jer 31:9).[7]

In Rabbi Meir's parable Israel is the wayward son of the king
(God) who is too ashamed to 'return' to God. By contrast, in
Jesus' parable there are *two* sons. One is the 'lost' son, representing
the 'sinners' Jesus was welcoming and with whom he was eating,
and the second is the judgmental brother, representing the
Pharisees who condemned Jesus for eating with sinners. Again,
Jesus' implicit identification of himself with the father (God)
welcoming the lost son (by eating with sinners) and admonishing

his brother (representing the Pharisees) was probably also outrageous and offensive. Jesus' sharp point is that the (repentant) 'sinners' are being welcomed by God but the (unrepentant) 'righteous' are the 'lost' ones.

I conclude that Jesus' parables of the lost are a sharp rebuke to the 'righteous' (the Pharisees), the more so when we consider that he radically changed traditional stories to do so.

No less vehement was his condemnation of the temple authorities (the Saduccees). In his parable of the tenants (Mark 12:1–12), based partly on Isaiah 5:1–7, Jesus portrays God as the owner of the vineyard (Israel), who fruitlessly sends various 'servants' (the prophets) to receive rent from the 'tenants' (temple authorities). Finally, the owner sends his 'beloved son', whom, however, the tenants kill. By this parable Jesus declared that the 'time' was, indeed, 'fulfilled' and, having been 'sent' as the 'son' of the owner of Israel, Jesus continued but also abrogated the former order.

The challenge of life in the kingdom

At heart, life in the kingdom of God means a close relationship with the Father, whose kingdom it is. God hears and answers the prayers of his children, as Jesus teaches in the parable of the father and his children (Luke 11:11–13; Matt. 7:9–11). Nonetheless, as Jesus teaches in the parables of the friend at midnight and the unjust judge, those children are to persevere in prayer and not be daunted by apparently unanswered prayer (Luke 11:5–8; 18:1–8).

Grace is fundamental to Jesus' kingdom, though it is not 'cheap grace', as Bonhoeffer famously called it. 'Sinners' are not saved because they are sinners anymore than the 'righteous' are lost for being righteous. 'Sinners' are saved because they are typically more ready to admit their need before God, as Jesus teaches in the parable of the Pharisee and the tax collector (Luke 18:9–14).

Many of Jesus' parables challenge his hearers to take his words with the utmost seriousness. In the parable of the soils, those who listen to his kingdom message are likened to various kinds of earth into which his words fall and who are exhorted to 'hear' him with attentive, open ears (Mark 4:1–9, 24–25). Inevitably, therefore, as he teaches in the parables of the two ways, the two trees and the two builders, his words divide the hearers into those who walk by the narrow way to life and those who walk by the broad way to destruction, between the fruitful and the fruitless, and between the wise and the foolish (Matt. 7:13–25).

Jesus gives these warnings because belonging to the kingdom of God is to be prized above all things, whether one stumbles upon it, as in the parable of the priceless pearl, or finds it after diligent search, as in the parable of lost treasure (Matt. 13:44–46). So incomparably secure is the kingdom in contrast with the insecurity of life that only a fool sets his hopes on wealth, as Jesus teaches in the parable of the rich fool (Luke 12:13–21).

Nonetheless, those who embrace the kingdom of God should do so only after careful reflection. In his parables of the tower builder and the warring king, Jesus warns his hearers to count the cost of following him and not to do so lightly (Luke 14:28–33). Messiahship is infinitely costly to Jesus and discipleship is likewise expensive to those who follow him.

Since grace is the basis of belonging to the kingdom of God, those who have entered are called upon reciprocally to be forgiving to their fellow members. As those forgiven much by God they are called upon to forgive the relatively little they have suffered from others. This Jesus teaches in the parable of the two debtors (Luke 7:41–50). Humility towards God and one's fellows, likewise, is the way of the kingdom of God, as in Jesus' parable of the humble servant (Luke 17:7–10). Jesus' parable of the good Samaritan radically redefines love to neighbour in a story where a hated Samaritan shows practical love to a Jew in a situation where his fellow Jews 'passed by on the other side' (Luke 10:31). On the other hand, his parable of the rich man and Lazarus teaches the culpability of a rich man who does nothing for the poor man 'at his gate' (Luke 16:20). Forgiveness, humility before God and man, practical care for a fellow human being regardless of race and religion lie at the heart of kingdom behaviour.

The end of the kingdom

The kingdom of God began with Jesus' preaching, accompanied by his controversial exorcisms and welcome of the unrighteous lost. The kingdom will reach its end just as abruptly, at the return of the Son of Man. The entire kingdom time line from beginning to end is captured in Jesus' short parable of the seed growing secretly:

> The kingdom of God is as if a man should scatter seed upon the ground, and should sleep and rise night and day, and the seed should sprout and grow, he knows not how. The earth produces of itself, first the blade, then the ear, then the full grain in the ear. But when the grain is ripe, at once he puts in the sickle, because the harvest has come. (Mark 4:26–29; see also the parable of wheat and tares, Matt. 13:34–43)

This parable is an allegory of kingdom history. It begins with Jesus, the sower of the seed of the kingdom message, and ends suddenly with the kingdom harvest when 'at once' he wields the sickle. In the related parable of the mustard seed, there is a similar contrast between the apparently small and undramatic beginning of the kingdom (Jesus and his small band of apprentice-preachers) and its massive end (a large tree that shelters the birds of the air, probably a reference to the ingathering of the Gentiles; Mark 4:30–32). That end, when it comes, will be like a bright light suddenly brought into a darkened room, revealing all things, as in the parable of the lamp (Mark 4:21–23).

Jesus teaches the suddenness of the appearing of the kingdom in several parables: the thief in the night, the night-time returning householder and the wise and foolish maidens (Matt. 24:22–24; Mark 13:34–36; Matt. 25:1–13). In each parable Jesus enjoins alert watchfulness, since no one knows when the thief will come, the householder will return or the bridegroom will arrive. It may be no coincidence that each parable, like the parable of the lamp, has an evening setting: darkness symbolizes evil times.

The advent of the kingdom of God will mean judgment of its members for their stewardship of their resources, in particular their generous use of money for the poor. In his parable of the wise steward, Jesus is referring to the auditing of a steward for his honest and wise distribution of a master's resources to his household servants. In his parallel parable of the dishonest steward, Jesus warns of the inevitable assessment of all members of the kingdom if they have been dishonest in distributing their master's money (see Luke 12:41–46; 16:1–3). Related to the notion of financial assessment is Jesus' parable of the talents (Matt. 25:14–30). Before his absence the wealthy man had distributed varyingly large amounts of money for business purposes (a 'talent' was equivalent to twenty years' wages for a labourer). On his return the lender will assess those lent the 'talents' according to their entrepreneurial enterprise. In short, members of the kingdom will be assessed at the end according to their honesty and wisdom as 'stewards' of the master's resources and their resourcefulness in the pursuit of 'kingdom' business.

The emphasis on evaluation is strongly present in the parable of the sheep and the goats (Matt. 25:31–46). Here, though, it is not the members of the kingdom who are being judged, but the people of the nations for their welcome or otherwise of the suffering messengers of the Messiah.

Jesus casts the revelation of the kingdom of God in positive terms in his parable of the wedding banquet (Matt. 22:1–14). Jesus makes many references to the end-time banquet of the Messiah (e.g. 25:1–12; Mark 2:19; Matt. 8:11; Luke 22:18).

Messiah in the parables

Do the parables of the kingdom tell us anything about Jesus, their teacher?

Who else except a messianic figure could teach such authoritative parables about so serious a subject as the kingdom of God? By contrast, the parables of the rabbis, as we have them, do not imply the divine interruption of the kingdom of God. Their parables are merely commentary on existing, unchanging pastoral aspects of second-temple Judaism. Jesus' parables, however, belong to the trajectory of salvation history, fulfilling the old order and initiating a new order that will be consummated at the final revelation of the kingdom of God. The parables' authoritative manner tell us that their teacher is the Messiah.

Furthermore, Jesus' messiahship is implicit in various images that echo the imagery of the Lord in the Old Testament.

References in Jesus' parables to the bridegroom, the shepherd and the rock, which Jesus applies to himself, appear intentionally to identify him with the Lord (Mark 2:19//Isa. 62:5 [bridegroom]; Mark 14:27//Ezek. 34:15 [shepherd]; Matt. 7:24–27//Isa. 28:18 [rock]). I reasonably conclude that Messiah Jesus saw his role with the people of the kingdom of God as functionally equivalent to the role of the Lord God with the people of the former covenant. This was not, however, somehow to replace the Lord, but to establish himself as the Lord's anointed king ruling on his behalf over the people of the kingdom.

Striking, however, in Jesus' parable of the bridegroom is his reference to the impending death of the bridegroom and the grief of the wedding guests 'on that day' (Mark 2:19–20). The parable gives no hint about the reason or circumstances of the bridegroom's death, only that it was in the future. By contrast, Jesus' parable of the tenants is explicit, both regarding Jesus' identity and the circumstances of his death (Mark 12:1–12). As to his identity, he is the 'beloved Son' (Mark 12:6) of the owner of the vineyard (the Lord) and its heir, and his death is the direct consequence of the tenants' rejection of his rights of ownership.

In sum, the authoritative nature of the kingdom parables implies messianic status of the teacher, and convey both implicitly and explicitly his messiahship as the filial Son who was to meet his violent death at the hands of the temple leaders.

Question of history

Given the sheer number of parables recorded in the Gospels, we can scarcely doubt that Jesus taught parables. True, their precise historical settings may be hidden from us by the way they have been included and shaped by the Gospel-writers. Yet their essential historicity and bold, if simple, messages remain secure. The Gospel-writers had such a profound respect for their Lord and Master that to tamper with his teachings would have been unthinkable.

Furthermore, the strong polemical tone of the parables of the strong man and the evil tenants point to the deadly enmity towards Jesus respectively by Pharisees and temple hierarchs. These parables reinforce our sense of the historicity of the broad narratives of the four Gospels, where his death occurs at their hands.

As we consider the parables overall, we discern a fundamental time line with a beginning, an end, and time-space in between. This permits us to think about the kingdom of God proclaimed by Jesus as a kingdom that supersedes and abrogates the old order. The kingdom Jesus initiated brings profound challenges to those who embrace it, and he will bring it to an abrupt, unheralded end when he is Judge of all. It will also issue in the wedding banquet of the Messiah. Clearly, where Jesus is, there the kingdom of God is.

My argument is that the parables of the kingdom of God are strong historical evidence that Jesus was the prophesied Messiah, both before his death and after his resurrection. This is a logical and intellectually satisfying conclusion based on reasonable historical analysis of the dozens of parables in the Gospels. Furthermore, and of great importance, it explains why and how the early Christians very soon came to worship him as Lord in their meetings. It was not that he was something else, something less, beforehand, whom later they irrationally began to worship and invoke. That indeed would make no sense at all, for crucifixion was a scandal to Jews.

8. MESSIAH'S MIRACLES

In an earlier chapter I pointed to the extensive evidence for Jesus' descent from king David, thereby qualifying him to be the long-awaited Messiah the prophets had promised. However, there must have been numerous other descendants of David in Israel and the Jewish diaspora at that time. But two other factors qualified Jesus to be the Messiah: the voice of God in the Jordan, 'you are my beloved Son' (Mark 1:11; my tr.), and his miracles.

Role of miracles

In the Gospels of Matthew, Mark and Luke the miracles of Jesus are evidence of his true identity as the messianic instrument of the kingdom of God:

> But that you may know that the Son of Man has authority on earth to forgive sins . . . I say to you, rise, take up your pallet [bed] and go home. (Mark 2:10–11)

> If it is by the finger of God that I cast out demons, then the kingdom
> of God has come upon you. (Luke 11:20)

Jesus' healing of the crippled man (Mark 2:10–11) was the proof
that he was God's authorized agent on earth to forgive sins, something only God had the right to do. In effect, Jesus is claiming that,
in forgiving sins, God is with and in him.

His casting out of demons (Luke 11:20) pointed to the divinely
appointed moment when God's kingdom was concretely and
immediately present in him in the here and now.

In John's account the miracles are evidence that the Father is
present in the Son: 'The words that I say to you I do not speak on
my own authority; but the Father who dwells in me does his works.
Believe me that I am in the Father and the Father in me; or else
believe me for the sake of the works themselves' (John 14:10–11).

Jesus' 'works' (miracles), like his 'words', are exercised under the
authority of the Father and point to the obedience and humility of
the Son. Whether in Matthew, Mark and Luke, or in John, the miracles of Jesus point to his unique identity as God's Son, his authorized
representative on earth and bearer of the kingdom of God.

Miraculous times?

'Jews demand signs', wrote Paul in commentary on his nation's
interest in the bizarre and inexplicable (1 Cor. 1:22). Jesus is likewise on record warning about his generation's preoccupation with
'signs' (Mark 8:11–12; Greek, *sēmeia*). Contemporary Jewish attitudes are evident in Josephus' fascination with portents (Greek,
terata) at many points; for example, in overnight storms, weird phenomena in the heavens or mysterious happenings in the temple
(*Jewish War* 4.287; 6.288–300; 6.292). Though an intelligent man
and an observant Jew, Josephus was deeply influenced by portents
and signs.

Paul, Jesus and Josephus are referring to what were superstitious
interpretations of natural phenomena that were in some way unexpected or unusual. Contrary to popular beliefs, however, actual

references to 'miraculous events' and 'miracle cures' among the Jews in the New Testament era are relatively rare in the surviving records.

Following are some of the more prominent miracle-workers from the era of Jesus:

1. The rabbi Honi the Circle-Drawer, also known as Onias (first century BC; Josephus, *Jewish Antiquities* 14.22), was said to have prayed successfully for rain, not merely a downpour or a drizzle but 'a rain of grace' (Mishnah, *Ta'anith* 3.8).[1]
2. John the disciple drew Jesus' attention to a man who was casting out demons in Jesus' name (Mark 9:38). It was not the *fact* of the exorcisms but that they were done in Jesus' name that caused John's comment. Josephus reports witnessing a Jewish exorcist named Eleazar drawing a demon through a man's nostrils and consigning it to a basin of water (*Jewish Antiquities* 8.46–49). Evidently, exorcisms were not unheard of nor exceptional.
3. Rabbi Gamaliel, the teacher of Saul of Tarsus, once prayed during a storm at sea, whereupon the sea subsided (*Babylonian Talmud Baba Meṣi'a* 59b).
4. In the AD seventies the rabbi Hanina ben Dosa prayed for the dangerously ill son of his teacher, Yohanan ben Zakkai, and the boy lived (*Babylonian Talmud Berakot* 34b).

To summarize, when the evidence for miracles in Jesus' times is investigated, they prove to be relatively infrequent, apart from exorcisms. Nonetheless, despite the relative rarity of reported miracles in Jesus' era in Israel, the suspicion remains with some people that the Gospel-writers invented miracles and attributed them to Jesus as a miracle-working man of his times.

The miracles of Jesus

When we turn to the Gospels, the *sheer number and variety* of Jesus' miracles are extraordinary. Mark reports no fewer than *eighteen* miracles, the majority of which are reproduced in Matthew and Luke. Found only in the source common to Matthew and Luke (Q) are *two* miracles, Matthew's special source (M) has *three*, Luke's special source (L) has *seven* and John has *six*.[2] In other words, five independent sources report about forty miracles of Jesus. Clearly, miracles represented a critical aspect of Jesus' ministry.

The miracles of Jesus were not 'contrary' to natural patterns: freakish or bizarre like the 'signs' and 'portents' the Jews sought. His miracles were restrained, done for the good of those in need and not as spectacles in the manner of magicians. They served to point to Jesus as at one with the Creator in revealing in advance his generous, end-time purposes on earth. In the miracles of Jesus, the kingdom of God was present among people as the Son of Man went about doing good.

Exorcisms

Jesus' exorcisms and the exorcisms of the disciples and others are prominent in the Gospel of Mark (1:23–27, 34, 39; 3:11–12, 22–30; 5:1–20; 6:7, 13; 7:24–27; 9:14–29, 38–41). The rationalist approach is to explain this as the product of the ignorance of pre-medical thinking. The notion of a world of spirits, it is argued, is no longer sustainable and possession by spirits can be explained scientifically.

It is true that some of the 'possession' described in Mark manifested itself in behaviour as an illness that today we would identify as schizophrenia or epilepsy (Mark 9:14–29; cf. Matt. 17:14–18; 5:1–20). The Gospels do attribute some sicknesses to demonic activity (e.g. Matt. 9:32–34; Luke 13:11). At the same time, however, most of the 'possession' in Mark is expressed as supernaturally inspired hostility to Jesus and opposition to the advent of the kingdom of God (Mark 1:23–27; 3:11–12, 22–30; 5:1–20). The rationalizing of all 'possession' as illness attributable to natural causes does not explain this profound supernatural opposition to Jesus.

Jesus' approach to exorcisms was different from his attitude to healing the diseased and disabled. He does not appear to have sought out sick people, though he invariably attended to those who came to him. By contrast, Jesus deliberately confronted the demon possessed. His deliverance of them was a visible sign of the nearness of the kingdom of God. Unlike the exorcists of his day, however, Jesus did not employ magical or mechanical means or call upon God in prayer. Rather, Jesus cast out the spirits authoritatively as God's anointed instrument of the impending rule of God on earth. Jesus' exorcisms pointed onward to his saving death, by which he was to liberate the subjects of the satanic kingdom.

Although the twelve cast out demons in their mission (also as a striking activity to accompanying their announcement of the kingdom of God), there is little evidence that exorcism was widely practised in early Christianity. The casting out of demons appears to have been especially associated with Jesus' unique ministry.

Evidence

Should the miracles of Jesus as the Gospels record them be regarded as historical? Several considerations give us grounds for confidence. First, there is evidence of Jesus' miracles in the non-Christian sources Josephus and the Talmud. Josephus, writing in the nineties, clearly intends us to understand that Jesus performed miracles when he states that 'Jesus . . . wrought surprising feats' (Josephus, *Jewish Antiquities* 18.63; Greek, *paradoxōn ergōn*).[3] The Talmud, written much later, says, 'they hanged Yeshu' because 'he practised sorcery' (*Babylonian Talmud Sanhedrin* 43a),[4] a probable reference to the accusation that he performed exorcisms by the power of the devil (Mark 3:22).

Secondly, the apostle Peter refers to the miracles of Jesus in his two major speeches recorded in the Acts of the Apostles:

Jesus of Nazareth, a man attested to you by God with *mighty works and wonders* and signs which God did through him in your midst, as you yourselves know . . . (Acts 2:22)

God anointed Jesus of Nazareth with the Holy Spirit and with power; how *he went about doing good and healing all who were oppressed by the devil* . . . (Acts 10:38)

Like the crowds in Jerusalem, the Roman centurion Cornelius, based in Caesarea Maritima, had doubtless heard of the remarkable deeds of Jesus (Acts 10:37).

Thirdly, some scholars find the *sayings* of Jesus about miracles particularly significant, especially those able to be retroverted into Aramaic. Consider, for example, Jesus' reply to the messengers from John the Baptist in prison:

> Go and tell John what you have seen and heard:
>> the blind receive their sight,
>> the lame walk,
>> lepers are cleansed,
>> and the deaf hear,
>> the dead are raised up,
>> the poor have good news preached to them.
>
> (Luke 7:22//Matt. 11:4–5)

Joachim Jeremias, an authority on Aramaic, argues that these words originally occurred in a speech rhythm characteristic of the way Jesus spoke.[5] In what is certainly a *saying* of Jesus, he appeals to what has been seen and heard in respect to miracles of healing the blind, the lame, the lepers, the deaf and raising the dead.

Another example is a saying cast in poetic form but set in the specific situation where Jesus sends a message to Herod Antipas, tetrarch of Galilee (whom he calls 'that fox'):

> Go and tell that fox,
>> 'Behold, I   cast out demons
>> and   perform cures
>> today and tomorrow,
>> and the third day I finish my course'.
>
> (Luke 13:32)

The poetry and sense of mystery indicate that this text is a genuine utterance of Jesus.

Likewise poetic is Jesus' pronouncement of blessedness on the disciples:

Blessed are the eyes which see what you see!

For I tell you that many prophets and kings

desired to see what you see,

and   did not see it;

and to hear what you hear,

and   did not hear it.

(Luke 10:23–24//Matt. 13:16–17)[6]

The poetry, parallelism and sense of fulfilment mark this text out as authentic. The ears of the disciples have heard Jesus' teaching and their eyes have seen his miracles of healing and exorcism.

Finally, in another passage common to Matthew and Luke (Q), Jesus says:

Woe to you, Chorazin!

woe to you, Bethsaida!

for if the *mighty works* done in you

had been done in Tyre and Sidon,

they would have repented long ago . . .

And you, Capernaum . . .

(Luke 10:13–15//Matt. 11:21, 23)

Once more, in a logion that appears to be historical, Jesus appeals to miraculous events that, by common agreement, happened in Chorazin, Bethsaida and Capernaum.

It is difficult to account for these various miracle sayings unless they corresponded in some way with Jesus' actions.

Fourthly, there are many examples of multiple attestations to exorcism, nature miracles, healings and the raising of the dead spread across the primary Gospel sources Mark, John, Q, L and M, as in the table below.

A wide range of miracle types is thus attested independently in the sample above. According to Barry Blackburn, 'the miracle-working activity of Jesus – at least exorcisms and healings – easily passes the criterion of multiple attestation'.[7] J. P. Meier, who devoted five hundred pages to reviewing Jesus' miracles, declared their multiple attestation to be 'massive'.[8]

	Mark	John	Q	L	M
Exorcism	Capernaum demoniac (1:21–28) Gerasene demoniac (5:1–20)				The dumb demoniac (9:32–34; cf. 10:5–8)
Nature Miracles	Stilling the storm (4:35–41) Feeding the five thousand (6:30–44) Walking on the water (6:45–52)	Feeding the five thousand (6:1–13) Walking on the water (6:16–21)		Draft of fishes (5:1–11)	
Healing	Withered hand (3:1–6) Blind Bartimaeus (10:46–52)	Official's son (4:46–54) Man born blind (9:1–34)	Centurion's boy (Matt. 8:5–13)	Bent woman (13:10–17)	
Resurrection	Daughter of Jairus (5:21–43)	Lazarus (11:1–44)		Widow's son (7:11–17)	

Scholars are divided over the question of the historicity of Jesus' miracles as reported in the Gospels.[9] Among those who doubt their truth is Norman Perrin, who asserts we cannot 'accept the necessary authenticity of any single story as it stands at present in the synoptic tradition; the legendary overlay and the influence of parallel stories from Hellenism and Judaism on the tradition are too strong for that'.[10] More positively, Jeremias observes that 'even when strict critical standards have been applied to the miracle stories, a demonstrably historical nucleus remains. Jesus performed healings that astonished his contemporaries.'[11] Based on his extensive review of scholars' opinions Blackburn concludes that the view that 'Jesus acted as an exorcist and healer can easily be described as *the consensus* of the modern period'.[12]

Conclusion

The numerous miracles of Jesus were different from the portents so prized in those times. His miracles provided confirmation that the long-awaited day of the Lord had come with the activities of the divinely commissioned Messiah.

9. MERCIFUL MESSIAH

Since evidently the early Christians worshipped Christ, the question must be asked, 'What manner of man was this exalted Christ before his crucifixion?'

One school of thought answers by claiming (a) that pagan cults were the defining influence for the Christian 'Christ cult', and (b) that Jesus of Nazareth was in reality a mundane person. In short, this viewpoint sees a radical *discontinuity* between the pre-paschal Jesus and the post-exalted Christ.

My argument, to the contrary, is that both claims are wrong. That is to say, (1) there is no evidence that pagan cults shaped earliest Christian worship, and (2) there is credible historical evidence that Jesus of Nazareth was *anything but* a merely mundane figure.

In relation to point 2 above, there are strong reasons for believing that Jesus saw himself as the Messiah of Israel (see earlier, pp. 81–82), that his followers reached that same conclusion, and that his execution for blasphemy as 'king of the Jews' by the Romans at the insistence of the Jews is best explained as their response to his messianic claims. That he redefined Messiah as *the* Son of Man, filial Son of God and Suffering Servant does not alter the core reality of his messianic consciousness and claims. Profoundly, Jesus believed that he had *been sent* by God and that he had *come* with a specific divinely mandated mission, convictions expressed by powerful actions like his ride up to the City of David and his clearing of the vendors from the temple.

These and other elements related to Jesus emerge across a number of independent sources underlying Matthew and Luke. Thus, by the principle of multiple witnesses, we are assured of being on firm historical ground. Jesus of Nazareth was a messianic figure, so that there is no disjunction between his pre-crucifixion person and the worship of him following his exaltation.

Yet this portrayal of Jesus is only partial. Taken on its own, Jesus' sense of identity and mission may come across as somehow bloodless and unrecognizable to the rest of us ordinary people. However, many glimpses of Jesus from his words and actions reveal his compassion and mercy.

John the Baptist and Jesus the Messiah

As prophets of the Lord, both the Messiah and his forerunner John the Baptist addressed the people of Israel as a whole. Moreover, both announced the nearness of the kingdom of God that was accompanied by the solemn call to 'repent' (Matt. 3:2 [John]; Mark 1:14–15 [Jesus]). John was visited by multitudes who streamed out to him from Jerusalem and Judea to the Jordan River. Greater crowds, however, came to Jesus in Galilee (from Galilee, Judea and Jerusalem, Idumea, from beyond the Jordan, and from around Tyre and Sidon) to hear Jesus and to seek healing from various diseases and disabilities (Mark 1:5 [John]; 3:7–8 [Jesus]).

There are at least three important differences between John and Jesus: (1) John rejected the messianic role, (2) performed no miracle, and (3) engaged with the crowds, not individuals. John dealt with the crowds globally, as it were, whereas Jesus also related extensively to individuals. In fact, many of the episodes in the Gospels are about Jesus' relationships with individuals, many of whom were severely disadvantaged in some way, whether through hunger, disease or disability. The Gospels record Jesus' compassion for these folk, none of whom was ever turned away (Mark 1:41; 6:34; 8:2; 9:22; Matt. 20:34; Luke 7:13). The central message in the parables of the good Samaritan and the welcoming father is that both showed unexpected compassion (Luke 10:33; 15:20). But both were, in reality, self-portraits of Jesus himself.

Messiah's emotions

Five times Mark states that Jesus 'looked right around', as in a circular sweep. On a number of occasions that looking around was to express anger (Mark 3:5; 11:11), sorrow (Mark 3:34) or severity (Mark 10:23). Apparently, there was something in Jesus' manner of looking that etched itself into the memory of his disciples.

Several times John refers to Jesus being 'troubled' (literally, 'agitated'). Jesus was 'troubled' when confronted with the grieving Martha and 'wept' (John 11:33, 35), and was further 'deeply affected' at Lazarus' tomb (John 11:38). He was likewise 'troubled' at the prospect of his death and by his sense of betrayal by Judas (John 12:27; 13:21). Mark reports that Jesus told his disciples in the Garden of Gethsemane that his soul was 'very sorrowful, even to death' (Mark 14:34).

These passing references serve to fill out a more complete picture of Jesus the Messiah. True, he expressed a strong sense of identity and mission as the divinely appointed agent of God, yet he also revealed emotions of indignation, sorrow and deep distress.

Meekness, humility and serving

In one statement, Jesus invited the heavily burdened to come to him for rest, probably referring to those who laboured under the weight of the numerous laws of the Pharisees. Jesus exemplified his negative attitude to the multiplication of ritual laws by deliberately breaking them, whether sabbath-keeping or the requirements of fasting and ritual washings (Mark 2:23 – 3:6; 2:18; 7:1–5). The Pharisees repeatedly accused him of breaking the sabbath (Mark 2:24; 3:4).

Jesus not only acted unlawfully in challenge to the Pharisees' oppressive legalism, but as a master rabbi also invited disciples to follow and learn from him. Yet he did so on the basis of grace and kindness. (It was unusual for a rabbi to invite disciples to follow him, since it was usually the reverse process: a would-be disciple first approached a master rabbi.)

Matthew reports Jesus as saying to those he invited:

> Take my yoke upon you, and learn from me;
> for I am *gentle* and *lowly* in heart,
> and you will find rest for your souls.
> For my yoke is easy, and my burden is light.
> (Matt. 11:29)

This self-disclosure helps fill out our more complete understanding of the Messiah.

The man with a mission who was possessed of a clear sense of his messianic identity is '*gentle* and *lowly* in heart'. So influential were these characteristics of Christ that they were to become the hallmark of the disciples in the coming years (1 Pet. 3:4; Rom. 12:16; 2 Cor. 10:1). The pre-Damascus Paul was arrogant and proud, but as a man in Christ prized humility above everything else (2 Cor. 8:9; Phil. 2:1–8).

Closely connected with meekness and humility was an attitude of serving others:

> Whoever would be great among you must be your servant.
> For even the Son of Man came not to serve,
>   but   to be served,
>   and   to give his life a ransom for many.
> (Mark 10:44–45; my tr.)

He illustrated this by placing a child in the midst of the Twelve, declaring that 'If anyone would be first, he must be last of all and servant of all' (Mark 9:35). On the night of his betrayal and arrest he washed his disciples' feet, saying that he had given them an example they should follow, adding his call for them to love one another, as he had loved them (John 13:15, 34). In the congregations of the apostolic age, the humble serving of one another was to be paramount (e.g. 1 Pet. 4:7–11; Rom. 12:9–12, 15–16; 1 Cor. 8:1; Eph. 5:2). The apostles repeatedly recall the selflessness of Christ as an example for believers to follow (Rom. 15:1–3; 1 Cor. 10:33 – 11:1).

Friend of sinners

The two extremes in Jewish society were the 'righteous' (Pharisees) and the 'sinners' (those who practised despised trades like tax collecting). The Pharisees' agenda was to bring *all* the people into compliance with the ritual and moral requirements of the Pharisaic tradition in the belief that the messianic age of the kingdom of God would come only when all Israel kept the law of God. Deficient law-keepers were viewed with contempt by the 'righteous' as 'sinners' and seen as barriers against the arrival of the new age.

The 'righteous' spurned Jesus because he was a noted law-breaker, but also because he identified closely with the 'sinners', actually sitting at table with them and thereby affirming them before God (Mark 2:15–17 par.; Luke 15:1–2). The 'righteous' probably viewed him as the chief obstacle to the arrival of the kingdom of God. To Jesus the 'sinners' were the 'lost sheep of the house of Israel', whom he had come to seek, find and save (Matt. 15:24–25; Luke 15:3–7; 19:9–10).

Accordingly, the 'righteous' derisively called Jesus 'friend of tax collectors and sinners' (Matt. 11:19; Luke 15:1–2). Jesus' gracious attitude to the 'lost' among the sheep of Israel powerfully shaped the attitudes of the apostles in their grace-based attitude to the salvation of the Gentiles in the coming decades (e.g. Gal. 2:15–16).

Children of Abba in his kingdom

While the fundamental teachings about God in the Old Testament as the all wise, omnipotent, sovereign King and Judge remain in the teaching of Jesus, they are no longer at the centre. For Christ and his disciples through his teaching and example the God of Israel was first and foremost *Abba*, 'dear Father': 'At that time Jesus declared, "I thank thee, *Father*, Lord of heaven and earth . . ."' (Matt. 11:25).

For Paul, as for Jesus, the Lord as *Father* was now the central truth about God, both as to theology and relationship. This is evident throughout Paul's letters, including his 'benediction' of the Father near the beginning of 2 Corinthians:

> Grace to you and peace from God *our Father* and the Lord Jesus Christ.
> Blessed be the God and *Father* of our Lord Jesus Christ,
> the *Father* of mercies and God of all comfort,
> who comforts us in all our affliction . . .
> (2 Cor. 1:2–4)

The 'God and Father of the Lord Jesus Christ' is also 'our Father'.

A condition of entry to the kingdom of *Abba* God was to 'become like children' (Matt. 18:3). Once in that kingdom and a child of *Abba* it was as if the day of salvation had *already* come. Everything for the children of *Abba* in the fallen world ruled by Satan is now changed:

> *Fear not*, little flock,
> for it is your Father's good pleasure to give you the kingdom.
> (Luke 12:32)

> *Do not be anxious* about tomorrow,
> for tomorrow will be anxious for itself.
> Let the day's own trouble be sufficient for the day.
> (Matt. 6:34)

> *Ask, and it will be given you*,
> seek, and you will find;
> knock, and it will be opened to you . . .
> If you then, who are evil, know how to give good gifts to your
>   children,
> How much more will your Father who is in heaven
> give good things to those who ask him!
> (Matt.7:7, 11)

> I *thank* thee, Father, Lord of heaven and earth . . . (Matt. 11:25)

> Do you *think* that these Galileans [on whom the tower fell] were worse
> sinners than all the other Galileans . . . ? (Luke 13:3)

These words of Jesus the Messiah teach the child in his kingdom
(1) 'not to fear', (2) 'not to be anxious', (3) to 'ask . . . your heavenly Father' for his 'good gifts', (4) to *give thanks* to God, and (5)
not to regard *sufferings* as personal punishment.

Joachim Jeremias, an expert on rabbinic teaching, illustrates how
radical these teachings were.[1] In Jesus' day, God was seen as
remote; prayer was formalistic, discouraged for small matters and
seen to attract merit (salvation without merit was inconceivable);
and suffering was to be viewed as punishment for sins.

Wives

In the Judaism of the New Testament era, husbands one-sidedly
had the right to divorce their wives, based on the decree of Moses
in the Torah:

> When a man takes a wife and marries her,
> if then she finds no favour in his eyes
> because he has found some indecency in her,
> and he writes her a bill of divorce
> and puts it in her hand and sends her out of his house . . .
> (Deut. 24:1)

The rabbis debated the meaning of 'indecency' (Mishnah, *Giṭṭin*
9.10).[2] The school of Shammai said it meant 'unchastity', whereas
for the school of Hillel it was 'even if she spoiled a dish for him'.
Rabbi Akiba said, 'Even if he found another fairer than she . . .'
What is not in dispute was the ease with which a man could
dismiss his wife (also, if she was barren; Mishnah, *Giṭṭin* 4.8[3]). She,
however, could neither divorce nor voluntarily leave him.[4]

When the Pharisees asked Jesus, 'Is it lawful for a man to
divorce his wife?' (Mark 10:2), they appeared to be challenging his

well-known pro-woman attitude. But to articulate his viewpoint spelled danger for Jesus: (1) for contradicting Moses (as in Deut. 24:1), but also (2) for implicitly condemning Herod Antipas' 'constructive' dismissal of his first wife, the Nabatean princess (Josephus, *Antiquities of the Jews* 18.110–111).

Christ did not engage the rabbis in debate but directly abrogated Moses' original instruction, asserting instead, 'What therefore God has joined together, let not man put asunder' (Mark 10:9; cf. Gen. 1:27; 2:24). God joins a wedded couple together for ever. By this single utterance and its accompanying prohibition of remarriage (except in the instance of adultery, Matt. 5:32; 19:9) Jesus the Messiah secured a revolutionary protection for vulnerable wives from husbands who selfishly invoked Moses' decree and potentially forced the wives they divorced into destitution.

Paul the ex-Pharisee knew of and pastorally applied Christ's concern for the protection of women from the one-sided privileges men had in Jewish society (1 Cor. 7:10–11, 13).

Women

Alongside Christ's protection of wives was his recognition of women socially. Under Judaism, female children were not educated (although boys were); in the temple precincts they were denied access beyond the Court of Women; their appearance was effectively obscured by plaited coiffure; generally speaking, they were confined to the home and did not converse with men apart from family members; it was assumed they would not act as witnesses in court hearings.[5] Jesus, however, instructed a woman, conversed alone with a woman, was accompanied and supported by women and entrusted a woman to carry the message of his resurrection to men (Luke 10:38–42; 11:27–28; John 4:27; Mark 15:40–41 par.; Luke 8:1–3; John 20:11–18).

Paul followed Christ's radical affirmation of women. He accepted the hospitality and patronage of women (Acts 16:15; Rom. 16:2), and assumed without comment the rightness of women to be engaged in evangelism alongside him (Phil. 4:3) and to pray or prophesy in the assembly (1 Cor. 11:5). He probably entrusted the carriage of the letter to the Romans to Phoebe, the deacon, and in his list of proven mission co-workers and supporters in Rome mentions Prisca (first), Mary, Junia (an apostle), Traephena, Tryphosa, Persis and the mother of Rufus (also Paul's 'mother'; Rom. 16:1–7). Once again, we see Paul the former strict Pharisee with radically changed attitudes, and the changes most probably stem from Christ himself.

Rejection of theocracy

The temple authorities accused Jesus of strenuously opposing the payment of personal tax to the Romans (Luke 23:1). Ironically, this was the very crime for which the Romans had executed his fellow Galilean Judas two decades earlier. In his famous reply to the Pharisees' and Herodians' entrapment question, Jesus says, 'Render to Caesar the things that are Caesar's . . .' (Mark 12:17 par.). In this single word, Christ's injunction to pay the tax effectively rejected altogether the zealots' theocratic ideal and programme for Israel.[6]

There is strong evidence of early church teaching to disciples and the state that emerges from Romans 13:1–7 and 1 Peter 2:13–17. Jesus' teaching about forgiveness and his recognition of the right of the pagan Caesar to rule the faithful overturned the dominant zealot ideal for a theocracy as an expression of the kingdom of God.

The Messiah's death *for* others

During the post-resurrection epoch, the writers of the New Testament letters repeatedly speak of Christ's sacrificial death *for* others, in the vicarious and substitutionary sense (e.g. 1 Thess. 5:10; 2 Cor. 5:21; Heb. 10:12; 1 Pet. 2:21, 24; 3:18).

Paul refers to a body of teaching he 'received' that 'the Christ died *for* our sins' (1 Cor. 15:3). Likewise, he appeals to the tradition he 'handed over' to them that he had also 'received' regarding the institution of the Lord's Supper, where Christ declared that his body would be broken and his blood shed *for* them (1 Cor 11:23–26//Luke 22:19–20). These traditions Paul 'received' must have been formulated in Jerusalem by the original disciples, who derived their teachings from Jesus.

There is good evidence that Jesus interpreted his coming death as a sacrifice for the forgiveness and liberation of *many* (Mark 10:45; 14:24). Jesus appears to have taken upon himself the role and destiny of the Servant of the Lord in Isaiah 52:13 – 53:12. Noteworthy in the Greek version of this passage is that the Servant does not die vicariously *for* the people, but only on account of their culpable failure to recognize him. But strikingly, the letter writers of the New Testament insist that Jesus the Servant died vicariously for the people. The most probable explanation for this view is that Jesus interpreted his death as *for* others, which in turn powerfully influenced the teaching of his disciples. He was, after all, the 'friend of sinners', and not only the 'sinners' in Israel but those everywhere.

Conclusion

Jesus is a truly enigmatic figure, too complex and vast for the human mind to encompass. On one hand, he is assured about his identity as Messiah, who is also the Son of Man and the filial Son of God. Furthermore, he is relentless in the pursuit of his God-given mission. But then we discover one who is meek and humble, a servant of others, a healer of the sick, a friend of outcasts, one who protects wives and affirms women and, above all, who sees his destiny as to die vicariously for the *many*. The Messiah conforms to no formula nor fits into any known mould. On one hand, he powerfully exercises the authority of God in argument against the 'righteous', while, on the other, he sits with the 'sinners'. He is at the same time both authoritative and humble.

Here we catch another glimpse of one who immediately after death was worshipped as Lord, yet by people in the churches who were called upon to be, like him, both humble and loving in their dealings with one another.

There is thus no discontinuity between the pre- and post-crucifixion Messiah. On this side of the resurrection he was the Lord whom his people had come to worship, and on the pre-resurrection side he was the humble servant in Israel whom his people took as the paradigm and template for all human relationships.

10. MESSIAH WHO IS LORD

We are fortunate to know the earliest surviving words of earliest Christianity, and are doubly fortunate that we have them in Aramaic, the language of Jesus and of the first Christians: *Maran atha* ('O Lord, come [back]'; 1 Cor. 16:22).

Paul wrote these words at the end of his first letter to the Corinthians, circa 54. But why does he leave them in Aramaic, when he wrote the letter in Greek?[1] Most probably because his readers already knew their meaning from the time Paul had been there five years earlier, and they had become a customary part of the assembly's prayers together.

Origin of 'the Lord'

Yet the words *Maran atha* probably did not originate with Paul, when he came to Corinth, but earlier and elsewhere. The overwhelming likelihood is that the prayer was formulated for church use in Jerusalem, soon after the historic lifespan of Jesus.

Another key reference to 'the Lord' in this letter is found in Paul's mention of the Lord's Supper. This reference also goes back to formulated prayers of the earliest Jerusalem church, which would also originally have been in Aramaic. But Paul wrote them in Greek for the practical reason that it was a longer liturgical passage. It narrates at some length what happened at the Last Supper when the Lord directed his followers to remember his death in the breaking of the bread and the blessing of the wine cup (1 Cor. 11:23–26).

The key reference to the 'Lord' in the early Jerusalem *Maran atha* prayer and the Last Supper liturgy recorded in 1 Corinthians are strong evidence that the earliest Jewish disciples worshipped the recently crucified Jesus as *Lord*.

Centrality of the Lord in early preaching and worship

In fact, the preaching and worship of Jesus as 'Lord' quickly became core activities in early Christianity, as is evident in the following examples:

we preach . . . Jesus Christ as *Lord*. (2 Cor. 4:5)

if you confess with your lips that Jesus is *Lord* . . . you will be saved. (Rom. 10:9)

This focus on *Lord* calls for explanation. My argument so far has been that Jesus was the Messiah and that messiahship was the dominant idea associated with him in the Gospels. Jesus was convinced that he was the Messiah; his disciples came to recognize him as the Messiah; he rode up to Jerusalem as the Messiah; he was crucified as the Messiah. So how did it come about that the earliest Christians came to pray to him and to preach about him as *Lord*?

'Lord [God]' and 'the Lord' in the sacred writings

The clue is to be found in Jesus' exposition of Psalms 110 and 2.

In Psalm 110 David enigmatically refers to someone he calls 'my Lord' (Hebrew, *'ădōnay*), who is at the 'right hand' of the Lord God, who will 'shatter kings on the day of wrath' and 'execute judgment among the nations' (vv. 5–6). Clearly, David's 'Lord' is a king and a warrior. In Psalm 2, however, David *himself* is the Lord God's 'anointed' (Messiah), his 'king' who will 'make the nations [his] heritage' and 'break [the nations] with a rod of iron' (vv. 8–9).

How can we explain the apparent contradiction between Psalms 2 and 110? How can David call *someone else* 'my Lord' (in Ps. 110) when David himself does the *same things* as that Lord (in Ps. 2)? The Scriptures do not resolve this.

In the following centuries Jewish scholars wrestled with a related problem in Psalm 110. They rightly assumed that the Christ (Messiah) was the son (descendant) of David, based on biblical prophecy. Yet (as noted above) David himself in this psalm speaks about a person he calls 'my Lord' (meaning the Messiah) being at God's 'right hand'. Psalm 110 does not explain the riddle how David's 'son' the Messiah can also be his 'Lord' seated in authority at God's right hand. In Jerusalem, during the last week of his life, Jesus confronted the scribes with this question: 'How can David's "son" *also* be David's "Lord"?'

Only Jesus knew that *he himself* was the answer. He was the *son of David* destined to be exalted to God's 'right hand' as *Lord*. Before his resurrection, Jesus of Nazareth knew he was the Messiah, the son of David, who after the resurrection was to become the 'Lord'.

Jesus' own explanation of Psalm 110 identified him to his disciples as 'the Lord' at 'God's right hand'. For this reason, after his death, resurrection and exaltation, they immediately identified him as 'Lord' both in the prayer *Maran atha* and the liturgy for the Lord's Supper (both of which we encounter in 1 Corinthians).

Psalm 110 in the New Testament

Psalm 110 is the most widely quoted text in the New Testament. But we must understand that it was Jesus' own explanation of the riddle embedded in Psalms 2 and 110 that shaped the

understanding of the early disciples and through them the theology of the New Testament. Some examples illustrate this:

For David did not ascend into the heavens; but he himself says,

'The Lord [God] said to my Lord, Sit at my *right hand*,
till I make thy enemies a stool for thy feet.'
(Peter, in Acts 2:34–35)

Is it Christ Jesus, who died, yes,
who was raised from the dead,
who is at the *right hand* of God,
who indeed intercedes for us?
(Paul, writing to the Romans [8:34])

But to what angel has he ever said,

'Sit at my *right hand*,
till I make thy enemies
a stool for thy feet'?
(Anonymous writer to the Hebrews [1:13])

Jesus Christ . . . has gone into heaven and is at the *right hand* of God,
with angels, authorities, and powers subject to him.
(Peter, writing his first letter [3:21–22])

The identification of Jesus as 'the Lord' at God's 'right hand' in
Psalm 110 is both exceedingly early and also widespread. It is
improbable that unaided Jesus' disciples would have connected
him with this psalm. Doubtless, they were at first as baffled about
the psalm as the scholars had been. Historically, the most probable
explanation for their understanding of the psalm's meaning is to
be found in Mark's brief account of Jesus' question to the scribes,
and his implied answer: that he himself was the 'son of David'
destined to be 'the Lord'. Based on Jesus' own interpretation of
Psalm 110, the leaders of early Christianity subsequently referred
to Jesus as 'Lord', at God's 'right hand'.

Improbable alternatives

Broadly, this view has two explanations, as represented by two noted scholars. Rudolph Bultmann, a specialist in Graeco-Oriental religions, held that Jesus as 'Lord' postdates Jesus and arose in Antioch in Syria, where the word 'lord' had been applied to gods and demi-gods in pagan worship and the emperor cult.[2] Geza Vermes, an authority on Judaism, rejects this view in favour of a Palestinian explanation based on studies of *mar*, 'lord' (a merely honorific title).[3] Vermes concludes that 'Lord' meant nothing more than a respectful reference to, for example, a charismatic rabbi.

Both explanations fail on several counts. One is, as we have seen, the extreme earliness of the use of *mar* in earliest Christianity. 'Lord' was well established in earliest Palestinian Christianity by the time Paul came to Antioch in the middle forties. In any case, the ex-Pharisee is unlikely to have been influenced by pagan idolatry. The other objection is that mere analysis of the word *mar* ultimately proves little. The question that must be addressed is 'How did Jesus answer the conundrum implicit in Psalms 2 and 110?' His answer is plain in the early and widespread references in the New Testament to Psalm 110.

The great question

So we return to our question. If, as seems certain, the earliest disciples after the resurrection prayed to Jesus as 'Lord', that is, as a divinity, what does that imply about the pre-resurrection Jesus? If Jesus were merely a prophet or rabbi, how can we explain the early post-resurrection *worship* of him as 'Lord'?

By now it should be evident that Jesus was anything but (merely) a prophet or rabbi. Rather, he betrayed a profound sense of having been 'sent' by God to 'seek and to save the lost' and to do so as the herald and miracle-working bearer of the kingdom of God in fulfilment of the law and the prophets. Above all, he was the Messiah, God's anointed, the rightful heir of the line of David, Immanuel (God with us), the beloved Son of the Father. He envisaged that death would not end him, but foresaw himself fulfilling the exalted status as the heavenly Son of Man, the Lord seated at the right hand of God.

All this and more Jesus held to be true of himself before the resurrection. The resurrection of Jesus did not prompt his disciples to invent an identity for him that he had not already revealed to them. Rather, the resurrection confirmed to them that his messianic and filial identity were indeed endorsed by God. The logic of history demands this. To dismiss Jesus as something other, something less, is to leave unanswered the great question 'Why did the early Christians worship this man?'

But first he had to die.

11. MESSIAH'S MISSION

Jesus is an enigma, 'the man who fits no formula'.[1]

The Gospel of Luke and the Acts of the Apostles, connected works, see Jesus existing in two phases, pre- and post-resurrection. The same two-phase pattern is found between the other Gospels and the letters. The Gospels confirm that Jesus had a genuinely historical lifespan (phase 1) and the letters confirm that the early Christians worshipped him (phase 2). The huge questions, then, are 'How did this man in phase 1 come to be worshipped in phase 2, and what kind of man had he been?'

Many Christians are untroubled by these questions and merely follow the lead of their ministers in accepting the Bible without further reflection.

On the other hand, however, scholars of sceptical bent explain the worship of the early Christians as due to the influence of the worship of deities by pagan cults. First-phase Jesus, they say, must have been something else, *nothing but* a . . . They usually fill in the blank by expanding on some true but secondary aspect of Jesus, for example, that he was a rabbi or prophet, while downplaying his core persona as Messiah, who was both the Son of Man and the Son of God (see pp. 50–53).

The sceptical approach has several problems. First, is that the early Christian leaders were *Jews*, for whom the worship of anybody apart from the Lord God was anathema. Accordingly, we must set aside the theory that the first Christians were copying pagan cults in their worship of Christ as a deity.

A second difficulty is that the Gospels focus on the phase 1 Jesus as an entirely historical figure. Only relatively rarely do the Gospels speak of him prospectively, using phase 2 terms like 'the Lord'. One of the few examples is in John's narrative: 'Now when *the Lord* knew that the Pharisees had heard that Jesus was making and baptizing more disciples than John' (John 4:1; cf. Mark 2:28; 11:3 par.; Luke 7:13; 10:1; 11:39; 12:42; 13:15; 17:5, 6; 18:6; 19:8; 22:61; 24:34; John 13:14; 20:18, 20, 25, 28; 21:12).[2] Mostly, however, the Gospels speak about the phase 1 Jesus in phase 1, historical terms.

The third difficulty for the sceptic is the stubborn fact of multiple witnesses to the otherwise inexplicable identity of the phase 1 Jesus. As we saw earlier, the Gospel of Luke was woven together from at least three discrete sources, Mark, Q (a source common to Matthew and Luke) and L (a source found only in Luke's Gospel).

Consider the table below, where the special ways Jesus referred to himself are found in the three independent sources Luke wove together in writing his Gospel.

	Mark	Q	L
The Son of Man	2:10; 8:38	Luke 12:40 = Matt. 24:44	19:10
The Christ	8:29–31; 12:36; 14:61	[Luke 7:22 = Matt. 11:4–6]	[22:30]
The Son	13:32 12:6 (beloved Son)	Luke 10:21–24 = Matt. 11:25–27	
His Father	8:38; 14:36 (*Abba*)	Luke 10:21–24 = Matt. 11:25–27	
My Father			22:29

Historians, like juries, depend on evidence from more than one witness. We are very fortunate that the sources underlying Matthew and Luke can be identified, and isolated from the Gospels in which they are embedded. This means we can check the spread of evidence for a range of issues like those in the table. On strictly historical grounds, then, we are able to say that Jesus referred to himself as 'the 'Son of Man' and the 'Son' of his Father and that his followers addressed him as 'the Christ', a conviction Jesus also expressed.

This means that low-level identifiers like 'rabbi' or 'prophet' while not untrue are quite inadequate. Jesus' categories of 'Son of Man', 'the Christ' (Messiah) and 'Son of God' emerge from the sources underlying the Gospels. The sceptical approach to the phase 1 Jesus simply does not work.

So we are left with a high-level phase 1 Jesus who is realistically worshipped as the phase 2 Jesus, as in the book of Acts and in the letters.

Messiah with a mission: three stages

We may think of Jesus' ministry in three stages:

1. AD 28/29	Concurrent with John the Baptist	John 1 – 4
2. AD 29/32	Arrest of John, Jesus' teaching in Galilee, the call and mission of the Twelve	Mark 1 – 5
3. AD 32/33	From the feeding of the 5,000 until his death in Jerusalem	Mark 6 – 16 John 6 – 20

The first stage was between John's baptism of Jesus and the arrest and imprisonment of John. During this period, when Jesus called five of his disciples, his ministry was only semi-public. Jesus did not step out into the full blaze of public life until John was removed from the scene.

The second stage was between the arrest of John and the feeding of the five thousand in Galilee. Jesus proclaimed his message in public, both in the synagogues and in the open places to great crowds. During this period he called his full complement of the Twelve for their mission (on his behalf) to the towns of Galilee.

The last stage was between the feeding of the five thousand and his execution in Jerusalem. The attempt to make him 'king' in Galilee meant he was forced to travel in secret in territories beyond the reach of Herod Antipas, tetrarch of Galilee (John 6:15). Finally, Jesus moved to the holy city, where he was executed for blasphemy as 'king of the Jews'.

I have given this outline of Jesus' ministry for two related reasons. First, it is recoverable from the narratives of the four Gospels. Secondly, because many of the teachings of Jesus are especially appropriate to the various stages of that ministry. For example, Jesus did not publicly proclaim the nearness of the kingdom of God in stage 1 while John was still at large, nor (apparently) during the final stage. Again, his teaching to the Twelve about their mission was relevant in stage 2. During the final stage, Jesus spoke about his death and the disciples' life together afterwards. In short, the sayings of Jesus more often than not belong to one or other stages of his ministry.

Messiah's actions

Jesus took a number of deliberate and highly symbolic actions:

- He called and was accompanied by twelve disciples.
- He taught by means of parables, which he explained privately to his disciples.
- He cast out unclean spirits at the time he proclaimed the kingdom of God.
- He healed the diseased and disabled.
- He broke the sabbath, and his disciples did not fast or purify their hands.
- He ate at table with sinners and other outcasts.
- He miraculously fed five thousand at Passover season.
- He publicly entered Jerusalem at the next Passover in the manner of the Messiah.

- He cursed the fruitless fig tree.
- He cleared the vendors from the temple.

These deliberate and public acts signify that Jesus was purposeful in his relationship with the people of Israel. The actions on their own, however, leave us uncertain exactly what those purposes were. The words of Jesus must be studied to understand the meaning of the actions.

Messiah's words: apostle of God, the 'sent' one

The table below gives examples from the Gospel sources where Jesus says that he has been *sent*, that is, by God.

	Mark	*M*	*L*	*John*
Jesus *sent*	9:37; 12:6	Matt. 15:24	Luke 4:18, 43; 10:16; 13:34	3:17; 4:34; 5:23–38 *passim*, 6:29–57 *passim*, 7:16–33 *passim*, 8:16–42 *passim*, 9:4, 7; 10:36; 12:44, 45, 49; 13:16–20; 14:24; 15:21; 16:5; 17:3–25 *passim* 20:21

Once again, the spread of references across four independent sources makes it certain that Jesus believed and declared himself to be *sent* by God. Jesus understood that while prophets before him were sent by God, he was the last to be sent, as the Father's *beloved Son* (Mark 12:6; cf. Luke 13:34). To welcome Jesus is to welcome God, who sent him (Mark 9:37). Whereas prophets said, 'Thus says the Lord', and rabbis, 'Thus is it written', Jesus said, '*I* say to you' (e.g. Matt. 5:21–48). God was present in the declarative words of Jesus.

Furthermore, Jesus' *sent* sayings reveal his mission as shepherd to Israel; for example, 'I was *sent* only to the lost sheep of the house of Israel' (Matt. 15:24). This is an implied messianic statement, since Ezekiel had prophesied a Davidic figure who would be the shepherd of Israel (Ezek. 34:23). Again, we discern Jesus' sense of mission in his words 'I must preach the good news of the kingdom of God to the other cities also; for I was *sent* for this purpose' (Luke 4:43).

The numerous *sent* sayings in the Gospel of John emphasize Jesus' obedience to the will of the Father who sent him; for example, 'I can do nothing on my own authority; as I hear, I judge; and my judgment is just, because I seek not my own will but the will of him who *sent* me' (John 5:30). Jesus' *sent* sayings reveal his humility and obedience to God.

It must be regarded as a matter of historical fact that Jesus portrayed himself as the apostle of God, the *Sent One*. He spoke with final authority, not as the prophets, nor the scribes – his words were God's words.

Jesus' words 'I have come to . . .'

Another table (see below) demonstrates the spread of Jesus 'I have come to . . .' sayings.

	Mark	*Q*	*L*
'I have come to . . .'	1:38; 2:17; 10:45	Luke 12:51 = Matt 10:34	12:49; 19:10

Once again, we see the principle of historicity based on multiple independent sources. There can be no doubt that Jesus' speech was characterized by this deep sense of mission:

- I *came* . . . *that* I may proclaim the kingdom of God (Mark 1:38).
- I *came* . . . *to* call . . . sinners (Mark 2:18).
- The Son of Man *came to* seek and to save the lost (Luke 19:10).
- I *came* . . . *to* cast a fire upon the earth (Luke 12:49).
- The Son of Man *came* . . . *to* give his life a ransom for many (Mark 10:45).

The first four sayings relate to Jesus' mission to Israel, to proclaim the nearness of God's rule so as to gather and save the 'lost', the 'sinners' in the land. Yet this mission will be turbulent, bringing (metaphorically) a fire on the earth, a fire that was to fall first on him and then upon the nation Israel in the years to come.

The fifth saying, however, broadens Messiah's mission from the 'lost sheep of the house of Israel' (Matt. 10:6; 15:24) to the nations of the world. This is hinted at in Jesus' words 'a ransom for *many*' (Mark 10:45), where 'many' is a kind of biblical code for the people of the world, and not just Israel. On another occasion he says, '*many* will come from east and west and sit at table with Abraham, Isaac and Jacob in the kingdom of heaven, while the sons of the kingdom [Israel] will be thrown into the outer darkness . . .' (Matt. 8:11–12). Also, in the parable of the king's wedding banquet for his son, outsiders will be welcomed, since the local people invited will not come (Matt. 22:1–10). In short, Jesus anticipated that Israel would reject her Messiah-King, but that the Gentile people of the nations would later welcome him.

Calling of the Twelve

Jesus' calling, training and sending twelve disciples is a major part of the second stage of his Galilean ministry (see the table below). And it must be regarded as historically based, given the principle of multiple witnesses.

	Mark	Q	L	John
Call of twelve disciples	3:14, 16	Luke 22:28–30 = Matt 19:28	[22:30]	6:67, 70, 71 20:24

The number 12 has potent redemptive significance, representing the restored tribes of Israel. His calculated choice of twelve implied his claim upon the whole nation, with its twelve tribes, and is an implied assertion of messiahship. The sight of twelve men following one impressive figure must have created a great impact upon those who witnessed it.

The One who was to come

Nowhere is Jesus' messianic sense better revealed than in his reply to the question from the imprisoned John, 'Are you he who is to come, or shall we look for another?' (Matt. 11:3).

Consider Jesus' reply, which the messengers took back to John:

> tell John what you hear and see:
> the *blind* receive their sight
> and the *lame* walk,
> *lepers* are cleansed
> and the *deaf* hear,
> and the *dead* are raised up,
> and the poor have good news [the gospel] preached to them.
> (Matt. 11:4–5)

Jesus' words intentionally echo an oracle of Isaiah the prophet, which had long been recognized as a messianic prophecy:

> Strengthen the weak hands,
>   and make firm the feeble knees.
> Say to those who are of a fearful heart,
>   'Be strong, fear not!
> Behold, your God
>   will come with vengeance,
> with the recompense of God.
>   He will come and save you.'
>
> Then the eyes of the *blind* shall be opened,
>   and the ears of the *deaf* unstopped;
> then shall the *lame* man leap like a hart,
>   and the tongue of the *dumb* sing for joy.
> (Isa. 35:3–6)

Jesus is saying to John, in clearest terms, 'The messianic age has arrived; the Messiah, the One who was to come, is here.' The healing of the blind and the lepers, the raising of the dead and the proclamation of good news to the poor is the evidence.

Conclusion

The identification of sources Mark, Q, L and M underlying
Matthew and Luke is very important, since it allows us to isolate a
multiplicity of independent texts. These virtually establish that
Jesus spoke of himself as the Son of Man and the Son of God
and that he acted in strongly symbolic ways, including calling
twelve men to be with him. He spoke of himself as *sent* by God,
and having *come* to fulfil a number of saving acts for his people and
the nations. These references establish Jesus' messianic mission.

12. MESSIAH'S DEITY

Jesus challenges us, not only existentially but also historically. How are we to reconcile the deity figure (the Lord) the first Christians worshipped with an altogether human figure, the man from Nazareth?

We are on firm ground historically in asserting that the early Christians worshipped Jesus as Lord. The hostile source Pliny confirms the many New Testament references to believers singing hymns *to* the *Lord* Jesus Christ. So there are no real doubts about the worship of the Lord that was happening on this side of the crucifixion.

Our problem is this: What can we say about the figure of the further side of the crucifixion, the *man* Jesus? Reduced to fundamentals, there are only two options. One is that Jesus of Nazareth was (somehow) a deity figure before the resurrection so that it was entirely appropriate for the disciples to worship him after the resurrection. The other is that such deity recognition beforehand was inappropriate either because the original disciples were mistaken about him or that they set out wilfully to deceive.

There are many who pursue the second option. Geza Vermes is an example of a leading scholar who thinks the church creeds that speak about Jesus as a divine figure are wrong. It is not that Vermes is critical of Jesus; in fact, quite the opposite. In his influential book *Jesus the Jew* (first published in 1973), Professor Vermes writes glowingly about Jesus as 'second to none in profundity of insight and grandeur of character'. Yet he was not the Son of God as the creeds teach, nor a deity figure, but something essentially different and lesser, a 'just man . . . [a] helper and healer'.[1]

At the popular level, Dan Brown in *The Da Vinci Code* conveyed to his readers that Jesus was merely a 'mortal prophet' whom the emperor Constantine made into the Son of God at the Council of Nicea in AD 325. This is simply untrue historically! In the immediate years after Jesus, the New Testament authors refer to him as God (Rom. 9:5; Heb. 1:8; John 1:1). Paul's letters contain evidence 270 years *before* Nicea that Christians worshipped Jesus as God. Pliny's letter to his emperor, written 215 years *before* Nicea, reports that Christians expressed worship to Jesus, 'as if to a god'.

Nonetheless, aside from post-resurrection attitudes to Jesus as God, Brown speaks for many in dismissing the pre-resurrection Jesus as merely a 'mortal prophet'. In effect, Vermes and Brown agree that the man, Jesus of Nazareth, was not God.

So how should we view the pre-resurrection Jesus? Was he God? Did the early Christian writings followed by the Creeds get it right in saying that he was?

Enigma

Did Jesus ever say, 'I am God'? Had he done so he would have claimed that in coming to earth he had evacuated heaven, leaving God's throne in heaven empty, leaving no one there in control of life and history. Jesus did not make that claim outright.

Rather, Jesus claimed to reveal God *functionally, declaratively* and *relationally*.

In oblique ways Jesus claimed to *do things* God alone has the right to do. In one example, Jesus claimed to have the authority to forgive sins, the sole prerogative of God. He revealed that authority visibly by healing the man who was an invalid (Mark 2:5–12). In another example, Jesus said that to follow him was to be given eternal life, a gift God alone bestows (Mark 10:21). To follow Jesus was the same as to keep the law of God perfectly. Again, Jesus told the parable of the father (God) welcoming home the prodigal son to justify *Jesus'* table fellowship with lost sinners (Luke 15:1–2). In Jesus' parable, the prodigal's father (God) in giving a banquet for his lost son confirms *Jesus'* action in eating with sinners. In short, to see Jesus *doing things* is to see before one's eyes the actions of the invisible God as portrayed in the Bible.

By his words Jesus *declared* that the kingdom of God was imminent, but his actions in casting out unclean spirits and welcoming the lost revealed *immediately* that *he* was the divine agent of God's kingdom. God's kingly rule from heaven was active in Jesus' words and deeds on earth. Furthermore, he displayed the same divine authority in prefixing his weighty oracles with the solemn 'Amen, I say to you . . .' As mentioned earlier, prophets declared, 'Thus says the Lord' and rabbis said, 'It is written,' but Jesus spoke with the authority of God himself.

Jesus addressed God as '*Abba*, Father', expressing a presumptive intimacy towards God unheard of in the sacred writings and said to have been without parallel in Jewish piety. He spoke of himself as *the* Son and of God as *the* Father and claimed a unique relationship with the Almighty only he was authorized to extend to others (Matt. 11:25–27).

The deity of Jesus of Nazareth is revealed in these examples, but it was revealed obliquely, for those who had ears to hear and eyes to see.

Identification

The Gospels have many examples where Jesus identified his words and actions with those of the Lord God of Israel.

He is recorded as saying, 'Heaven and earth will pass away, but my words shall not pass away' (Matt. 24:35). Here Jesus echoes

Isaiah, who wrote, 'the word of our God will stand for ever' (Matt. 24:35; Isa. 40:8). The words of Jesus are as absolute as the words of God.

As mentioned earlier, in the course of his ministry Jesus described himself as the *bridegroom*, the *shepherd* and the *rock*, terms God applied to himself, as set out in the Scriptures (Mark 2:19//Isa. 62:5; Mark 14:27//Ezek. 34:15; Matt. 7:24–27//Isa. 28:16). These identifying images powerfully connect Jesus with God.

Most significantly of all, as we have seen, Jesus spoke of himself as 'I AM', recalling the high point in the Old Testament where God revealed himself to Moses and the people by these words (Exod. 3:14). Yet by these very words Jesus identified himself with God. 'Be not afraid, I AM,' he told the terrified fishermen, words that appear in independent sources (Mark 6:50; John 6:20; my tr.). Jesus refers to himself many times in the Gospel of John as 'I AM', in both absolute and qualified senses (e.g. 'I AM *the bread of life*'; John 6:35). But these I AM words also occur in the Synoptic Gospels; for example, when Jesus answered the high priest, 'I AM; and you will see the Son of Man seated at the right hand of Power . . .' (Mark 14:62). The false prophets imitate Jesus in saying, 'I AM', thereby confirming *his* use of these words (Mark 13:6).

Recognition

It is improbable that the disciples fully grasped the profound reality of Jesus' divine identity at the time. It took some time, the fact of the resurrection and the illumination of the Spirit to comprehend the deity of the man they had followed. After the resurrection, his words about the *Son of Man* present with God as the ruler of history and the *Lord at God's right hand* came into clearer focus. Accordingly, it was natural and right that they worshipped him and invoked his name for salvation in the ways I have been outlining.

Redefinition

In the era of the New Testament a prayer ('benediction') like the following, the first of the *Nineteen Benedictions*, was recited in the synagogues:

> Blessed art thou, O Lord and God of our fathers,
> God of Abraham, God of Isaac, and God of Jacob,
> great, mighty and fearful God, most high . . .[2]

It is interesting to contrast this with a benediction Paul wrote: 'Blessed be the God and Father of our Lord Jesus Christ, the Father of mercies and God of all comfort . . .' (2 Cor. 1:3)

As a strict Pharisee the pre-Damascus Paul would fervently have held to the truth of the synagogue benediction. Writing now as a Christian in his reworked benediction, he does nothing to detract from the conviction that the Lord was the God of his fathers Abraham, Isaac and Jacob. The radical thing, however, is that this God is now understood to be 'the God and Father of our Lord Jesus Christ' and, moreover, '*our* Father' (Matt. 6:9). In other words, the revelation of Jesus as Son of God has revealed what previously had been hidden, that the God of Israel is *Father* – the Father of the Messiah Jesus, and our Father.

The point is that this revelation of plurality within the being of God occurred *before* the resurrection. Once more we recall that Jesus referred to God as *the* Father and to himself as *the* Son (Matt. 11:25–27). That is, the idea of the Trinity was implicit in the words and actions of the pre-resurrection Jesus.

Once the resurrection was accomplished, the outlines of trinitarian thought began to appear, as for example in the words of the risen Jesus:

> All authority in heaven and on earth has been given to me.
> Go therefore and make disciples of all nations,
> baptizing them in the name   of the Father and
>   of the Son and
>   of the Holy Spirit . . .

(Matt. 28:18–19)

There is one 'name' (a synonym for God) that, however, is equally owned by the Father *and* the Son *and* the Holy Spirit. Somehow there is *threeness* within the unique *oneness* of God.

The Trinity

According to Paul:

> when the time had fully come,
> God *sent forth his Son*,
>> born of woman,
>> born under the law,
>>> to redeem those who were under the law,
>>> so that we might receive adoption as sons.
> And because you are sons,
> God has *sent the Spirit of his Son* into our hearts,
>>> crying, '*Abba! Father!*'
> (Gal. 4:4–6)

God revealed his triune character purposefully, (1) sending his *Son* to make those in bondage to law his sons, (2) sending *the Spirit* of his Son to his adopted sons, (3) to enable them to call God '*Abba*, Father'.

Paul is careful to preserve the temporal sequence. The Son God sent was 'born of a woman'; that is, he was that Son *before the resurrection*. God sent the Spirit of his Son *after the resurrection* to those who had already been redeemed and adopted. Thus the Trinity is not an abstraction to mystify us but an attempt to express a practical description of the way God has saved those lost from him. He sent his Son into the world and the Spirit of his Son into human hearts, so that they might know God as *Abba*, Father.

In the following centuries there were a number of struggles to comprehend the Trinity (though the word itself was not used until the early third century). In the second century the Egyptian Gnostics rejected the idea of the Son's genuine humanity. This viewpoint became known as Docetism, based on a word meaning 'to seem', because Jesus only *seemed* to be a man. During the next century, several church leaders proposed what is called Modalism, because God (being indivisible) had revealed himself in various temporary modes. There was no actual person called the Father, nor the Son, nor the Spirit. Early in the fourth century the Egyptian Arius taught that the Son was not eternal and did not belong to the inner being of God, being merely a time-bound extrapolation from God.

These problems prompted church leaders to sharpen existing catechetical summaries into what became known as the Apostles' and Nicene Creeds. Based on the New Testament, these state-ments of true faith taught (1) the true humanity of the Son of God, (2) the distinct persons of Father, Son and Spirit, and (3) the Son's equal deity with the Father.

Contrary to Vermes (the scholar) and Brown (the novelist) the deity of the Messiah was not an idea thought up centuries later. Rather, the deity of the Messiah was apparent prior to the resur-rection and as a matter of logic asserted in implicitly trinitarian terms soon after the resurrection. The explicit teaching of the deity of the Son as the second person of the Trinity in later years was in response to aberrant teaching, and flows out of and is entirely consistent with the New Testament.

Was Jesus God?

Historically, it is clear that the earliest Christians (Jews and monotheists) worshipped Jesus as Lord. That recognition and worship is consistent with their conviction that the man Jesus of Nazareth identified himself as *the* Son sent by *the* Father. Jesus, however, did not claim outright to be God in an absolute sense since that would have denied the reality of the One he called 'my Father'. Instead, Jesus asserted his deity and Sonship in a way that avoided Modalism.

13. SERVANT MESSIAH

I gave my back to the smiters,
   and my cheeks to those who pulled out the beard;
I hid not my face
   from shame and spitting.
     (Isa. 50:6)

The title of this chapter attempts to convey the truly astonishing paradox of Jesus of Nazareth. On one hand, he is the lofty figure who is the Messiah, the Son of God and the Lord. Yet, at the same time, he was humiliated by the rejection of his nation's religious leaders who handed him over to the Gentiles for execution.

As he makes his final fateful journey to Jerusalem Jesus asks, 'How is it written of the Son of man, that he should suffer many things and be treated with contempt?' (Mark 9:12).

The paradox is contained within this brief question, a summation of what was *written* in the sacred writings. At one extremity Jesus breathtakingly asserts he is *the* Son of Man, who according to Daniel 7:13–14 will come to the side of God in heaven to be given universal dominion. At the other, by contrast, he declares it to be *written* that this exalted One will first *suffer many things* and be *treated with contempt*.

Jesus, despised and delivered up

To which of the sacred writings was Jesus referring? Clearly, it was to Isaiah 53:3, where Jesus' exact word, translated as 'treated with contempt', appears, but translated in the Isaiah passage as 'despised':

> He was *despised* and rejected by men;
>   a man of sorrows, and acquainted with grief;
> and as one from whom men hide their faces
>   he was *despised*, and we esteemed him not.

This text belongs to a lengthy poem about a man the Lord God calls 'my servant' (Isa. 52:13 – 53:12).

So, in that journey to Jerusalem Jesus identifies himself as the Servant of the Lord about whom Isaiah prophesied. Twice more on that journey Jesus also echoes Isaiah 52:13 – 53:12, where he says he will be 'delivered', or 'handed over':

> The Son of man will be *delivered* into the hands of men,
> and they will kill him . . .
> (Mark 9:31)

> Behold, we are going up to Jerusalem;
> and the Son of man will be *delivered* to the chief priests and the scribes,
> and they will condemn him to death, and deliver him to the
>   Gentiles . . .
> (Mark 10:33)

The key word 'delivered' occurs in Isaiah 53:12 (Greek version). Jesus' echoing of this word must have become embedded in the memories of his disciples. It occurs again in the opening words of the early Jerusalem Last Supper formula, 'on the night when he was betrayed [*delivered*] . . .' (1 Cor. 11:23), and in the Jerusalem tradition Paul quotes in his letter to the Romans, 'He was *delivered* for our transgressions . . .' (Rom. 4:25, my tr.). I conclude, based on Isaiah 52:13 – 53:12, that Jesus understood it to be the will of his Father to be *treated with contempt* and *delivered* into the hands of the temple leaders, who would then *deliver* him to the Roman authorities for execution.

Angry reaction

Imagine the anger of the disciples when Jesus first speaks like this. At Caesarea Philippi they have just honoured him by calling him the Messiah, whereupon he immediately deflates their hopes by speaking of his impending shameful death:

> And he began to teach them that the Son of man must suffer many
> things,
> and be rejected by the elders and the chief priests and the scribes,
> and be killed . . .
> (Mark 8:31)

Once more in Jesus' words 'must . . . be *rejected*' we hear echoes from Isaiah 53:3, '*rejected* by men', and understand that this 'must' happen, as by an unalterable divine decree.

What madness was this? Every Jew expected the Messiah to be a triumphant 'new David', the Lord's anointed king to conquer the enemies of God and 'shatter' the kings of the earth, as Psalm 2 predicted. In more recent times writers prophesied that the Messiah would bring the kingdom of heaven to earth, whose world capital would be the temple-city Jerusalem, from where the law of God would extend to the ends of the earth. But Jesus, who has just now accepted he is the Messiah, speaks of his *rejection* and *death* in Jerusalem, the City of David.

We cannot easily imagine the shock and anger Jesus' words must have generated in the minds of those present that day at Caesarea Philippi. Twenty years later Paul observed that the very idea of a 'crucified Messiah' was a 'stumbling block to Jews' (literally a 'scandal' to them; 1 Cor. 1:23). In other words, for Jews like the disciples the promise of a Messiah meant victory and vindication for God's righteous nation, the expulsion of the hated Roman occupiers, the restoration of national pride as in the days of the conquests of their great king, David. It must have taken a huge sense of loyalty to Jesus as, in great confusion and fear, they followed behind him when he strode on purposefully to the holy city where (he said) humiliation, rejection and death awaited him at the hands of the Gentiles.

The Gospels convey something of the bewilderment of these men. Luke records a conversation between two of his followers after his burial. One says, 'We had *hoped* that he was the one to redeem Israel' (Luke 24:21). Even after the resurrection the disciples still hold messianic hopes. They ask, 'Lord, will you at this time restore the kingdom to Israel?' (Acts 1:6).

Before long, however, they come to understand his challenge to them at Caesarea Philippi. If his is to be the way of the cross (literally) so too will theirs be the way of the cross (figuratively) (Mark 8:34). That is, they must be prepared publicly to identify themselves as his followers, although this will mean sharing his rejection. The writings of the New Testament are infused with the notion that the sufferings of Christ will spill over to his people (see e.g. Rom. 8:35–37; 2 Cor. 1:5; 1 Pet. 4:13).

The Servant Poems

Isaiah's poem about the Suffering Servant of the Lord (52:13 – 53:12) is preceded by three similar though shorter passages (42:1–4; 49:1–6; 50:4–9) forming a cycle of Servant Poems that dominate Isaiah 40 – 55.

In these chapters Isaiah also refers to the nation Israel *collectively* as God's servant. But it is a negative reference. Israel the servant is 'blind' and needing to be delivered from her captivity (Isa. 42:19; 44:1–2, 21; 45:4; 48:20). In the four Servant Poems in the cycle, however, Isaiah points unmistakably to an *individual* Servant of the Lord who does not need to be redeemed but is the redeemer of Israel. This Servant, who is an individual, belongs to the nation Israel, but is her rescuer.

In the First and Fourth Poems the speaker is the Lord who addresses the servant as 'my servant'. In the Second and Third Poems, however, the speaker is the servant himself, who reflects on the Lord's words to him.

As we read these four Servant Poems, we are struck by the ways in which Jesus' sense of identity and purpose cohered with these texts.

First Poem

In the First Poem the Lord addresses the servant as

> my servant, whom I uphold,
> my chosen, in whom my soul delights.
> (Isa. 42:1)

We are immediately reminded that the voice of God addressed Jesus when baptized by John in the Jordan, 'You are my beloved Son in whom I am well pleased' (Mark 1:11; my tr.). Dominating everything we know about Jesus was his conviction that he was the *beloved Son* of the Father (Matt. 11:27; Mark 12:5).

Furthermore, Jesus taught his immediate disciples to know God as their Father, and the apostles likewise inculcated in the disciples throughout the world that the God and Father of the Lord Jesus Christ was also their Father. Jesus' reflection on the Servant Poems seems to have contributed significantly to his understanding that he was God's Chosen One who was bringing delight to the Lord.

Third Poem

In the Third Poem the Servant speaks of his *humility* as a teacher:

> The Lord GOD has given me
>   the tongue of those who are taught,
> that I may know how to sustain with a word
>   him that is weary.
> Morning by morning he wakens,

> he wakens my ear
>> to hear as those who are taught.
>> (Isa. 50:4)

The Servant is a teacher, but one who is himself humble as one who submits to instruction. Only then is he equipped to sustain the weary.

Consider Jesus' own self-revelation, where he declares himself to be 'gentle and lowly of heart' and invites the 'weary' to come to him and find 'rest' (Matt. 11:28–29). Humility, meekness and gentleness are repeatedly urged upon readers of the letters of the New Testament. These qualities are the marks of those who follow the way of Jesus.

In the same poem the Servant declares his unflinching obedience to God and trust in him in the face of terrible suffering:

> The Lord GOD has opened my ear,
>> and I was not rebellious,
>> I turned not backward.
> I gave my back to the smiters,
>> and my cheeks to those who pulled out the beard;
> I hid not my face
>> from shame and spitting.
>
> For the Lord GOD helps me;
>> therefore I have not been confounded;
> therefore I have set my face like a flint,
>> and I know that I shall not be put to shame . . .
>> (Isa. 50:5–7)

Jesus fulfilled the Servant's words in his resolute and determined final journey to Jerusalem. In Gethsemane, knowing the horrors that lay ahead Jesus prayed to his Father, 'Not my will but yours be done' (Mark 14:35–36; my tr.). Most probably the Father's will was confirmed to Jesus in the Servant's words.

Fourth Poem

In the Fourth Poem (52:13 – 53:12) we learn in particular of the sufferings of the Servant (also in Isa. 49:7; 50:4–9). We hear two

voices: the voice of the Lord and the voice of the people. The
dominant voice is the Lord's, speaking of his Servant's sufferings
but also of his ultimate vindication by God (Isa. 52:13–15; 53:7–
12). The other voice is *from the people* for whom the servant was to
suffer (53:1–6):

> [v. 1] Who has believed what *we* have heard?
> And to whom has the arm of the LORD been revealed?

> [v. 2] For he grew up before him like a young plant,
>   and like a root out of dry ground;
> he had no form or comeliness that *we* should look at him,
>   and no beauty that *we* should desire him.

> [v. 3] He was despised and rejected by men;
>   a man of sorrows, and acquainted with grief;
> and as one from whom men hide their faces
>   he was despised, and *we* esteemed him not.

> [v. 4] Surely he has borne our griefs
>   and carried *our* sorrows;
> yet *we* esteemed him stricken,
>   smitten by God, and afflicted.

> [v. 5] But he was wounded for *our* transgressions,
>   he was bruised for *our* iniquities;
> upon him was the chastisement that made *us* whole,
>   and with his stripes *we* are healed.

> [v. 6] All *we* like sheep have gone astray;
>   *we* have turned every one to his own way;
> and the LORD has laid on him
>   the iniquity of *us* all.

In verses 1–3 the people testify to the ugliness of the Servant's
humiliation and sufferings; but in verses 4–6, they say that these
sufferings were on account of *their* transgressions. More than that,
they say that the Lord 'laid on' his Servant the 'chastisement' of

their 'iniquities'. According to the Fourth Poem, the Lord made his Servant a vicarious sacrifice for the sins of the people.

On his way to Jerusalem and in the holy city on the last night Jesus applied the Servant's vicarious language to himself. The *fact* of the Servant's humiliation and death that Jesus applied to himself (noted above) he now *explains*. Those sufferings are for *others*:

> For even the Son of Man came not to be served but to serve,
> and to give his life as a ransom for many.
> (Mark 10:45, my tr.)

Once more, we see the paradox between so lofty a figure as the Son of Man and one whose very purpose in coming was to serve, and this by the gift of his own life as a ransom to liberate many captives. So exalted a figure might have come expecting others to serve him. But the opposite was to happen. *Even* the Son of Man came to serve, thus setting the example for all people everywhere to follow. The language of serving others by freeing them reveals Jesus' understanding of the Fourth Servant Poem. Especially noteworthy is the original word translated 'for' (Greek, *anti*), which means 'in place of', so that Jesus interprets his impending death as *substitutionary*, purchasing the freedom of 'many'. His offering of himself, the One for the 'many', echoes the drift of this poem.

On his last night, before his arrest, Jesus speaks these words as he takes the cup at the Passover meal:

> This is my blood of the covenant,
> which is poured out *for many*.
> (Mark 14:24)

His 'blood', represented in the wine cup, is to be 'poured out' in death. Jesus declares this death to be 'for many', once more echoing the Fourth Servant Poem. Here the word 'for' (Greek, *hyper*) means 'for the sake of' or 'for the benefit' of others. Once more, the death of the one will be for the sake of 'many', as in the Fourth Poem.

At that meal, Jesus institutes a simple ritual to teach people in coming generations that his death has been *for* them. After his

death the disciples formulate Jesus' instructions at the Last Supper
into a simple ritual, where the words of Jesus about his death *for*
others are to be repeated.

Paul reminds the believers in Corinth of the Last Supper and its
adjunct, the Lord's Supper:

> For I received from the Lord what I also delivered to you,
> that the Lord Jesus on the night when he was betrayed took bread,
> and when he had given thanks, he broke it, and said,
>> 'This is my body which is *for* you.
>>> Do this in remembrance of me.'
> In the same way also the cup, after supper, saying,
>> 'This cup is the new covenant in my blood.
>>> Do this, as often as you drink it, in remembrance of me.'
> (1 Cor. 11:23–25)

The frequent repetition of the Lord's Supper or Eucharist in
early Christianity was a constant reminder that his death was *for*
the people and helps explain how the death of Jesus as an aton-
ing sacrifice became so prominent in the writings of the New
Testament.

Paul also reminds the disciples in Corinth about the preaching
that created their church:

> I delivered to you as of first importance what I also received,
> that Christ died *for* our sins in accordance with the scriptures . . .
> (1 Cor. 15:3)

Paul did not invent this form of words but 'received' them, most
probably in Damascus when he was baptized. They originated in
Jerusalem soon after the death of Jesus.

This prompts an important question: 'Which "Scriptures" did
Christ's death for others fulfil?' The answer is, 'Part of the Fourth
Servant Poem, Isaiah 53:3–6.'

In Paul's references to the Lord's Supper and in the outline of
the early preaching we find clear references to the death of Jesus
for others. Paul 'received' these teachings from the earliest disciples
in Jerusalem, who in turn had 'received' them from Jesus. When

we ask where Jesus came to understand that his death was to be substitutionary and vicarious, we reasonably conclude that he learned it from Isaiah 52:13 – 53:12.

First and Second Poems

In the First and Second Servant Poems we learn that the Servant has a mission *first* to Israel and *then* to the nations:

> And now the LORD says . . .
> 'It is too light a thing that you should be my servant
>   to raise up the tribes of Jacob
>   and to restore the preserved of Israel;
> I will give you as a light to the nations,
>   that my salvation may reach to the end of the earth.'
> (Isa. 49:5–6)

The Lord directed Jesus through these words. Throughout his ministry Jesus concentrated on 'the lost sheep of the house of Israel', regarding it as God's will that he should bring the gospel of the kingdom *first* to the covenant people (Matt. 15:24; 10:5–6; Mark 7:27). As his end drew closer, however, he foresaw the spread of the gospel *next* to the Gentile nations (Mark 13:10; 14:9). In short, the two-beat mission the Lord gave to the Servant, Jesus took to be his own.

Significantly, however, the Lord gave special emphasis to the nations. Three times in the First Poem he commissions his servant to take his 'justice' to the nations (Isa. 42:1, 3, 4). His manner of doing so will be consistent with his humility, obedience and sufferings as in the other poems. He is a herald who does not speak, a reed bruised but not broken and a smouldering wick that does not burn (Isa. 42:2–3).

Soon after Jesus' historic lifespan, Saul the persecutor became a disciple. He was no ordinary believer, however, but one convinced God had called him to become the apostle to the Gentiles. Saul, later known as Paul, devoted the remaining years of his life to this calling. He was deeply aware of the Servant Poems in Isaiah:

God . . . has shone in our hearts to give the *light* of the knowledge of the glory of God in the face of Christ. (2 Cor. 4:6)

> I will give you [my servant]
> as a *light* to the nations,
>   that my salvation may reach
> to the end of the earth.
> (Isa. 49:6)

Paul was convinced that God had shone in his heart (at Damascus) so that, in turn, he was able to give that light to the people of the nations. Paul actually saw himself as 'the light to the nations', though in a derived and dependent sense, since the true light to the nations was the Servant, Jesus (Acts 13:47; 26:17, 23). Paul established the pattern and practice of missionary vocation outside Israel. Yet Jesus did this beforehand and did so (in part) under the impulse of the Poems of the Servant.

Identity and vocation

Many have (rightly) recognized the role of these Servant Poems in Isaiah 40 – 55, especially in the words of Jesus during his final journey to Jerusalem as well as in the holy city. Jesus made his own the words and teaching of these poems. He was assured that he was (1) God's Elect Beloved, (2) who was to follow the path of humility and resolute obedience in suffering and death, (3) for the redemption of the many, and (4) who thereby would bring God's justice to the nations.

Inevitably, this raises the question about the source of Jesus' identity and mission. Was Jesus solely dependent on the text of Isaiah (and other Scriptures) or did he know *within himself* that he was the Son of God and the Servant of God? Did these ideas come to Jesus by instruction or by intuition?

Our difficulty is that of limited information. From the observations of this chapter we conclude that Jesus' own reflection on biblical texts was extremely formative (see p. 71). On the other hand, however, we know that the boy Jesus in the temple *already* knew that God was his Father, whose set course he was bound to follow (Luke 2:49). At the same time, however, that incident reveals this boy's remarkable knowledge of the Scriptures that enabled him to engage on equal terms with learned scholars. Our conclusion, then, is that Jesus knew within himself who he was and the nature of his calling. Yet we must also conclude that he was confirmed and strengthened in this by his immersion in the text of the sacred writings, among which the Poems of the Servant of the Lord were highly significant.

14. RESURRECTION

Jews of the second temple period believed the dead would rise from their graves at the end of history, as prophesied by Ezekiel (Ezek. 37:1–14). They also believed that occasionally the spirits of deceased persons could live on in still-living people, though the origin of this idea is obscure. For example, people then thought that Jeremiah or other prophets from the past somehow animated Jesus and that the now-dead John the Baptist was at work in the mission of the twelve disciples (Matt. 16:14; cf. Mark 6:14). But the people in Jesus' day definitely did not believe an individual would rise up bodily from the grave ahead of the universal resurrection at the end of history. Resurrection was for the end time, but not beforehand, as Martha told Jesus (John 11:24).

Indeed, when the ex-Pharisee Paul spoke about the resurrection of Jesus, he did so on the basis that it was part of the end-time universal resurrection. This he said had actually begun when Jesus was raised; he was 'the first fruits of those who have fallen asleep' (1 Cor. 15:20). As Paul understood it, the general resurrection had commenced but had been suspended for the time being to be resumed and completed at some propitious moment in the future.

The apostle likened the resurrection of Jesus to a harvest that had been started but then halted for a period, before being resumed and finalized.

The risen and exalted Christ had confronted Paul on the road to Damascus so that Paul was compelled by what he had seen and heard to believe Jesus had been resurrected. However, when Jesus told the original disciples he would be put to death but then raised alive on the third day, it was as if they had not heard him (Mark 9:10; cf. John 9:10). His words fell on deaf ears. They simply did not comprehend that an *individual* dead person would be raised independently of and prior to the universal resurrection.

It took the accumulated realities of the empty tomb and the appearances of Jesus in tangible bodily form to convince them that God had raised him, an individual, from the dead. Otherwise, they might have felt they were imagining he was alive, as it were in their subjective consciousness, perhaps as a kind of wish fulfilment induced by their tragic sense of loss. But no, the tomb was *empty*; they had touched his body, eaten with him and seen the wounds in his hands and feet. The texts leave us in no doubt: it was a physical, bodily resurrection.

The evidence for Jesus' resurrection falls into four categories: Paul's direct testimony, his citation of the Jerusalem resurrection tradition he had 'received', the appearances traditions in the Gospels, and the Jerusalem oral tradition and the Gospel sources.

Paul's direct testimony

Paul boldly asks the rhetorical question 'Have I not seen Jesus our Lord?' (1 Cor. 9:1), by which he means Christ's encounter with him on the road to Damascus. On at least sixteen occasions Paul refers to or alludes to the Damascus event as the turning point in his life.[1] The book of Acts narrates this event no fewer than three times (Acts 9:1–19; 22:4–16; 26:9–20). True, Paul mentions his 'out-of-the-body' experience when caught up to the third heaven where, however, he 'heard things that cannot be told' (2 Cor. 12:1–9). By contrast, near Damascus, God revealed his Son to Paul for one specific purpose: to *preach* him to the Gentiles (Gal. 1:15).

The Damascus road event was for Paul a resurrection appearance when he both saw and heard the Lord; it was no mere 'vision' or 'revelation' like the one he related to the Corinthians, as above.

In 1 Corinthians 15:8 Paul expands upon his earlier reference to having 'seen the Lord' when he refers to himself as the one 'last of all' to whom the risen Lord appeared: 'Last of all, as to one untimely born, he appeared also to me.'

Paul makes this bold statement as a conclusion to his list of apostles to whom the Lord appeared. The thing to note is that the distinctive reality Paul and the apostles before him have in common is that, having seen the Lord, they proclaim the same message of the crucified and risen Lord. Paul needs to make this point to the Corinthians, since some of them do not believe in the possibility of resurrection. He asks, 'how can some of you say that there is no resurrection of the dead'? (1 Cor. 15:12).

Paul's testimony 'Have I not seen Jesus our Lord?' is different from the appearances of the Lord to the apostles before him (see below). Whereas the original witnesses saw the risen Lord within a thirty-seven-day period, in Paul's case it was a year or so after the ascension that he 'saw' him (Acts 1:1–3). Paul *saw and heard* the Lord, but differently, as the unusual words 'as to one untimely born' imply.

The effects of this distinction are considerable. For Paul it meant he was seen as a second-class apostle, one who had *not* been a disciple of Jesus and who had *not* actually seen and handled the Lord in the way the others before him had.

For us, however, this distinction is very important historically, since it means the original disciples did not see and hear Jesus from heaven as Paul later did, *but on earth*, in Jerusalem and in Galilee. In other words, the distinction Paul makes reinforces the fact that the original Jerusalem witness to Jesus' resurrection was not from heaven (as it was for Paul) but on earth physically, concretely and bodily. Clearly, those today who say the resurrection of Jesus was just 'in the minds' of the disciples are wrong.

Although Paul's encounter with the risen Christ was different from the apostles before him, it was nonetheless a genuinely resurrected Jesus he saw and heard. His words 'Have I not seen Jesus our Lord?' refer to the Lord who had been raised bodily, but was now also exalted to heaven.

Paul's reference to the resurrected Christ as 'first fruits' of the resurrection harvest requires a resurrection of *his body*, because the end-time resurrection, of which the first fruits was an anticipation, will be of the *bodies* of all people. Since that final universal resurrection will be bodily, the resurrection of Christ as its first fruits was likewise a bodily resurrection and no mere vision either of the original disciples or Paul.

Paul's citation of the Jerusalem resurrection tradition

The earliest historical reference to the resurrection of Jesus is found in Paul's quotation circa 54 of an oral statement he had 'received' either in 34 (at his baptism in Damascus) or 36 (from Cephas in Jerusalem), which had been formulated in Jerusalem beforehand,[2] very soon after Jesus' death in 33 (1 Cor. 15:3–7):

> what I . . . received
> that   Christ died for our sins
> > in accordance with the scriptures
>
> that   he was buried
> that   he was raised on the third day
> > in accordance with the scriptures, and
>
> that   he appeared to Cephas,
> > then   to the twelve.
> > Then   he appeared to more than five hundred brethren at the one time,
> > > most of whom are still alive,
> > > though some have fallen asleep,
> >
> > Then   he appeared to James,
> > then   to all the apostles.

This passage had probably been created originally in Jerusalem as a memorizable teaching aid (the fourfold *that* followed by the fourfold *then* suggests an original catechetical format).

This carefully rounded statement introduced by '*what* I received' signifies something objective, an entity, a raft of four facts, each introduced by *that*.[3] Each *that* in effect introduced a separate statement that today we would place within quotation marks (Greek then lacked punctuation marks). In other words, this oral teaching contains four critical assertions from the earliest believers in Jerusalem.

But the four statements are logically interconnected: Christ died *and* was buried *and* was raised on the third day *and* appeared alive to various people. The four statements are of a piece, forming one complete statement about what happened to Christ at the time of the first Easter. He died, was buried, was raised and appeared. Each statement depends on its predecessor: Christ appeared *because* he had been raised; he was raised *because* he had been buried; he was buried *because* he had died.

Having died, Christ was not so much 'buried' (downwards, as in a grave) but *entombed* (sideways, in a tomb hewn out of rock; cf. Acts 13:29).[4]

He was *raised* on the *third* day. Paul's Greek here betrays an underlying Aramaic form of words; literally, 'Christ . . . was raised *in the day the third*.' Paul's uncorrected Greek echoes the confession of the Aramaic-speaking community in Jerusalem from whom he had received it.

He appeared on five occasions, the 'then . . . then . . . then . . . then' suggesting precise sequence. The first two probably occurred in Jerusalem, the third and fourth in Galilee and the fifth in Jerusalem.

The names of those to whom he appeared (and was seen by) are either given (Cephas/Peter, the Twelve, James) or are able to be readily ascertained (the five hundred, all the apostles). The witnesses to this event can be interrogated, including the vast number of five hundred who saw the risen Christ on one occasion. The sources of this remarkable event are identified and accessible. Let those who doubt go and inquire of these people themselves.

Paul states that this fourfold *that*, whose focus is the resurrection sightings, is what he and the Jerusalem apostles preach and what the churches believe (1 Cor. 15:11). Clearly, the fact of Jesus' resurrection was absolutely central in early Christianity.

The appearances traditions in the Gospels

The Gospel of Mark

Mark does not narrate any appearance of the risen Lord. Rather, he recounts Jesus' declaration of his coming resurrection during his final journey to Jerusalem, words that fell on the disciples' deaf ears (Mark 8:31; 9:31; 10:34; cf. 9:9–10). They were mystified about the Messiah's resurrection both because (1) resurrection was to be universal, occurring on the far distant horizon as the climax of history, (2) they could not come to terms with the idea of the *death* of the Messiah, and (3) the sacred writings were silent about the Messiah's resurrection. For Jews at that time, Messiah was entirely mundane and applicable to this material world. We must dismiss any idea that the disciples later made Jesus fit in with a precise prophecy of the resurrection of the Messiah, for there was none.[5] As already mentioned, the only resurrection Jews then knew of was the resurrection *of all people* at the end of history (as in Ezek. 37).

Despite the absence of direct narrative, however, Mark intends his readers to know about the bodily resurrection of Jesus.

First, Jesus states that 'after' he is 'raised up' he will meet them again in Galilee (Mark 14:28). This implies a literal resurrection from the dead in Jerusalem, after which he will go to Galilee to meet them.

Secondly, when the women come to the tomb early on the first day of the week, they find it empty – Jesus' body is not there. At the entrance to the tomb a young man speaks to them:

> you seek Jesus of Nazareth, who was crucified.
> He has risen; he is not here;
> see the place where they laid him.
> But go, tell his disciples and Peter that he is going before you to
>   Galilee;
> there you will see him, as he told you.
> (Mark 16:6–7)

Mark may intend us to understand that the young man is an angelic messenger, since he is dressed in a white robe. He explains that the emptiness of the tomb is because Jesus is 'risen' and is 'going before' them to Galilee, where they will see him.

These words find their place in Mark's narrative because the women must have recounted them later to the disciples. As many have observed, this is remarkable, since the witness of women was not admissible in court proceedings (see p. 100).

We can only speculate as to Mark's reasons for failing to provide direct narrative of the disciples' encounter with the risen Lord. Perhaps he intends to heighten the mysterious in Jesus by baldly introducing him without warning or information about his early life, and making him disappear similarly. Whatever the reason, he leaves us in no doubt about the fact of Jesus' resurrection.

The Q source

The source common to Matthew and Luke (called Q) is a collection consisting mainly of Jesus' sayings. It broadly follows the chronology of Mark, but tails off before Jesus reaches Jerusalem so that there is an absence of narrative reference to Jesus' death and resurrection.

We may only guess the reason. Did Q originally have a Jerusalem section, but Matthew and Luke decided not to employ it since they already had an extended Jerusalem narrative in Mark's Gospel?

Nonetheless, Jesus' sayings in Q expect that he will be raised from the dead. The theme of future resurrection in 'Q' is found in both implicit and explicit references.[6]

1. Jesus' words about the patriarchs and believers seated at table in the kingdom while those watching gnashed their teeth implied the notion of a coming resurrection and final judgment (Luke 13:28–29//Matt. 8:11–12). Likewise, the Q saying of John the Baptist about raising up children for Abraham makes sense only from a setting where the coming general resurrection was believed (Luke 3:8//Matt. 3:7–10). Again, Jesus' promise that his followers will sit upon thrones judging the twelve tribes presupposes future resurrection and final judgment (Luke 22:30//Matt. 19:28).

2. Jesus explicitly speaks of his own coming resurrection as the 'sign' of the prophet Jonah. As Jonah was a 'sign' to the men of

Nineveh, so one greater than Jonah, the Son of Man, will be in his generation. That 'sign' (explicit in Matt. 12:40, implicit in Luke 11:31–32) points to Jonah's escape after three days from the belly of the great fish and points to Jesus' escape from the heart of the earth by resurrection after three days.

In sum, the Q source quotes Jesus affirming both the future general resurrection and his own personal resurrection.

The L source

According to Luke's opening words, the original disciples (who became 'servants of the word' after the resurrection) handed over to him various written traditions, which he combined to create his Gospel. We don't know when and where Luke received these texts, whether in Antioch in the forties, Palestine in the late fifties or Rome in the early sixties. More important is his observation that the original disciples-become-apostles handed these writings to him.

Among these texts was L, which like Mark and Q appears to follow the broad and well-known sequence of Jesus' public ministry, beginning in Galilee and ending in Jerusalem. L concludes with an extensive account of Jesus' resurrection appearances (recounted in Luke):

24:8–11	The women tell the disciples that the tomb was empty.
24:12	Peter finds the tomb empty, but is mystified.
24:13–33	Jesus appears to two men walking to Emmaus, who report this to the disciples.
24:34	Disciples reported that the Lord had earlier appeared to Peter.
24:36–48	Jesus appears to the disciples in Jerusalem.

Like Mark, L assumes the tomb was empty but adds the detail of Peter visiting the tomb to find it empty. L has the lengthy narrative of two disciples who meet the risen Jesus and who report this to the disciples in Jerusalem. The appearance of these obscure men points to the genuineness of the text; a contrived account would have involved well-known disciples. Jesus' subsequent appearance to the gathered disciples occurred at mealtime and his act of eating with them established the reality of his *physical* resurrection.

The M source

The Jewish tone of the M source points to a Jewish and Palestinian origin, though details of the date and place elude us. The greater part of M consists of Jesus' teachings and parables. The few narrative sections cluster around the death and resurrection of Jesus.

The M source picks up Mark's account of the women finding the tomb empty and narrates that Jesus himself appeared to them as they were returning home. He instructs them to tell the disciples to go to Galilee, where they will meet him.

When the disciples come to Galilee, Jesus meets and directs them to 'go' and 'make disciples of all nations' (Matt. 28:19).

The Gospel of John

The Gospel of John stands apart from Matthew, Mark and Luke and their underlying sources. This Gospel is the written version of a separate oral tradition stream.

In John's account Mary of Magdala and other women come to the tomb, find it empty and report this to the disciples. Peter and John then come to the tomb and find only Jesus' burial cloths. Mary returns to the tomb, where the risen Jesus speaks to her, requesting that she not hold on to him physically and directing her to report his words to the disciples.

Three accounts follow of the risen Jesus appearing to his disciples. The first is on the evening of that first day of the week (Sunday) inside the room in Jerusalem where the disciples are hiding, with Thomas missing. The second occurs the following Sunday evening when Thomas is present and Jesus demonstrates that his resurrected body is corporeal. The third appearance is lakeside in Galilee, where Jesus prepares breakfast for the seven fishermen.

Sequence according to Gospel sources

Luke comments that the period between Jesus' 'passion' and being 'taken up' is forty days (Acts 1:2–3).

On the first day in Jerusalem

1. Mark (followed by L and M) and John narrate that named women come to the tomb early on the first day of the week and find it empty. The body is not there.
2. The L source and John indicate that Peter then comes to the tomb, also finding it empty. In John, the beloved disciple comes with Peter.
3. There is an instruction that the risen Jesus is to meet the disciples in Galilee – by a young man (so Mark) or by Jesus himself (so M).
4. The risen Jesus appears to Peter (L).
5. The risen Jesus meets two disciples on the road to Emmaus.
6. The risen Jesus comes to the disciples on that first evening in Jerusalem (so L and John).

A week later in Jerusalem

7. The risen Jesus meets them a week later in Jerusalem (so only John).

Some days later, in Galilee

8. Jesus meets the disciples in Galilee – at the lake (John) or on a mountain (Matthew).

Forty days after the crucifixion, in Jerusalem

9. Jesus bids them farewell in Jerusalem (so L).

Whether directly or indirectly, all the sources indicate that Jesus' resurrection is no mere apparition, but a bodily corporeal reality.

The Jerusalem oral tradition and the Gospel sources

It is impossible to harmonize the sequence of appearances of the risen Jesus as we have them in the early Jerusalem tradition (quoted by Paul) and in the independent Gospel strands in John, L and M. Nonetheless, the table below gives some indication of the frequency of the appearances throughout those thirty-seven days.

While the precise sequence is uncertain, we may say that, to our knowledge, the risen Christ appeared on at least *eleven* separate occasions to individuals and groups. He was seen, heard and touched at different times and places, establishing that his resurrection was bodily. The names of those to whom he appeared are either given or readily ascertainable.

The difficulty harmonizing the underlying sources has been highlighted as evidence of unreliability. It should be mentioned, however, that the Gospel writers are not setting out to prove or even to narrate the history of Jesus' resurrection appearances systematically. These authors write from the assumption that their readers know about and believe the resurrection. As noted, the

1 Corinthians 15	John 20	Luke 24	Matthew 28
Jerusalem			
	Mary		
			Women
[Christ] appeared to Cephas		Simon 2 disciples	
next, to the Twelve	10 disciples 11 disciples	Disciples	
Galilee	7 disciples		
next, to 500+			Disciples in Galilee
next, to James *Jerusalem* next, to all the apostles		Disciples	

earliest and most complete narrative is the Jerusalem oral tradition quoted by Paul. If we make that our starting point, we find that some elements in the Gospel sources fit in well; for example, Jesus' appearances to Peter, then to the twelve, then to all the apostles.

Furthermore, the very existence of 'loose ends' is evidence that these writers have not contrived a harmonious, even account. The discrepancies are a reason to believe in the innocent integrity of the writers and, indeed, are usual in writers of the period. Three historians who narrate the Great Fire of Rome in AD 64 disagree about Nero's whereabouts during the fire and whether he 'fiddled' (played the lyre) or sang while the city burned. But no one doubts that Nero failed to show leadership while the inferno almost destroyed the city.

In short, the resurrection appearances of Jesus to so many people and at different times and places as recorded in the oral tradition and the Gospel sources argues powerfully for the truth of the resurrection.

Circumstantial evidence

In addition to evidence based on Paul's direct testimony, his citation of the Jerusalem tradition and the independent traditions in the Gospel sources there is circumstantial evidence.

References to resurrection in the letters are gratuitous

The term 'gratuitous' may be applied to references to the resurrection in the New Testament letters. This is because the information about the resurrection of Jesus is not introduced to prove that it happened but rather on the assumption that it *had* happened.

This is not to say that the original hearers (whether Jews or Gentiles) would easily have accepted the resurrection of Jesus from the dead. Jews, as we have seen, were looking for a universal resurrection at the *end* of history. The resurrection of an individual before that momentous day, who was then permanently (as opposed to temporarily) alive would not have been understood. For their part, Gentiles of the Greek world believed in the

immortality of the soul after the decay of the body. The resurrection of the body would have struck them as decidedly odd. Some
of Paul's hearers in Athens, when they heard of the resurrection
of the dead, mocked him (Acts 17:32). Only powerful arguments
from the apostles could have convinced Jews and Gentiles to
become Christians on the basis that Jesus had been raised from the
dead. In itself it was neither a winning nor a credible message,
either in the culture of the Jews or of the Gentiles.

The letters of James and John do not make direct reference to
the resurrection of Jesus. But they do speak of his second coming,
which of course is presupposed by his resurrection (Jas 5:9; cf. 2:1;
5:15; 1 John 3:2). This indicates the degree to which both writers
and readers took Jesus' resurrection to be an established fact.

In his first letter Peter speaks of the resurrection of Jesus from
the dead as the basis of the believers' faith and hope and of their
forgiveness before God (1 Pet. 1:3, 21; 3:18, 21). But it is not something for which Peter has to contend; rather, it is given as a basis
for godly confidence.

The gratuitous nature of resurrection references is illustrated by
Paul's major reference to the resurrection of Jesus in 1 Corinthians
15:3–8, to which I have already referred. Paul is responding to a
report that some of the Corinthians have expressed doubts about
their own bodily resurrection. 'How can some of you say that there
is no resurrection of the dead?' he asks (1 Cor. 15:12). Paul corrects
this theological error by appealing to the given fact of the death,
burial, resurrection on the third day and subsequent appearances
of the risen Christ on a number of occasions. The Corinthians will
be raised from the dead because Christ *has been* raised from the
dead (1 Cor. 15:20–21). But the fact is not in doubt and does not
need to be argued. He is reminding them of something they already
know as a basis of getting their thinking straight on this issue.

I conclude that James, Peter, John and Paul as well as Jude and
the writer of Hebrews were convinced of the truth of the resurrection of Jesus (Jude 21; Heb. 1:3; 2:9; 13:20). Where did this
conviction originate? There is no special pleading, no propping up
of their case. The most reasonable explanation for their convictions is that they arose from fact, the fact that Jesus was *raised from
the dead.*

The changed lives of James, Peter and Paul

Three of those named as having seen the risen Christ (James, Peter and Paul) died as martyrs three decades after the resurrection. James was executed in Jerusalem AD 62 at the hands of the high priest, Annas II, while Peter and Paul died in Rome in the mid-sixties under the emperor Nero.

We are able to follow the life and movements of James and Peter over the previous thirty-five years, and those of Paul over the previous thirty years. The records are extensive.

Remarkably, these men, who were to become mission leaders as a result of the change the risen Christ had made in their lives, did not apparently know one another beforehand. Nor were they agreed about all things as leaders of the various mission teams. Differences of opinion, even quarrels among them, are a matter of record (cf. Gal. 2:11–14; 1 Cor. 1:12; 9:5; Acts 21:18–21). But they were united in their belief in and proclamation of the resurrection of Jesus (1 Cor. 15:5, 7, 8, 11).

Critical questions are posed by the lives of these men. Why did James, Jesus' younger brother, who did not originally believe in Jesus (John 7:5), *become* his devoted servant after the first Easter? Why did Peter *continue* to serve Jesus after his death, apparently having expected the apocalyptic kingdom of God to intervene when Jesus arrived in Jerusalem (Luke 22:38, 49; 24:21; John 18:10; Acts 1:6)? Why did Paul *begin and continue* to serve Jesus at such great personal cost, having first been a zealous persecutor of Jesus' followers (Gal. 1:13–16)?

The resurrection of Jesus from the dead is critical to these questions. Peter would not have continued, nor James and Paul begun, to serve Jesus unless these men were convinced Jesus had been raised from the dead.

James had remained in Nazareth with his brothers, sisters and Mary after Jesus moved to Capernaum to commence his public ministry in Galilee. Probably, he too had been an artisan like Joseph, his father, and his older brother, Jesus. There is evidence of resentment, or even hostility, towards Jesus (Mark 3:21, 31–35). Yet after the first Easter, James is found first as a member, then as the first of the three pillars, then as sole leader of the Jerusalem church (Acts 1:14; 12:17; 15:13; 21:18; Gal. 1:19; 2:9). James, who had been an unknown Nazarene, became leader of a community of many thousands in Jerusalem. Josephus' lengthy description of James's death points to his eminence in Jerusalem in the early sixties (*Antiquities of the Jews* 20.200).

Peter's changed life direction from that of an obscure fisherman in the landlocked Sea of Tiberias to that of sect leader in Jerusalem calls for explanation, as do his world travels from Galilee through Judea, Samaria, Syria, Asia Minor, Greece to Italy and also his authoritative encyclical to the Anatolian provinces.

Consider, too, the radical turnaround of *Saul*, the obsessive protector of the faith of his fathers, who, as a leading scholar and activist, sought to destroy the heretical sect associated with Jesus. But this man became the leading promoter of the sect he had attempted to obliterate and did so among the Gentiles, a people who, as a strict Pharisee, he would have despised for their idolatry and promiscuity. How can we account for this astonishing change? In his own words, it was because the Lord, who had been raised on the third day, appeared to him (1 Cor. 15:8–9).

James, Peter and Paul each served the risen Lord for about thirty years: James in Judea, Peter and Paul on the world stage. It is difficult to believe that they would have done this unless they were convinced that Jesus was, indeed, the risen Lord. Is it possible for *each* to have been so mistaken for *thirty* years? Remember that they were not members of a tight-knit group, but robust individuals who operated in separate missions and were often at odds with one another.

The moral tone of their letters suggests clear thinking and burning integrity, not delusion or deceit!

It might be argued that monks in eastern religions are prepared to die through self-immolation in the expectation of reincarnation, or that Islamic extremists will embrace suicide bombings for the bliss of Paradise. The leaders James, Peter and John, however, did not serve Christ and die for him in prospect of an unverifiable future life. Rather, they lived and died as they did on account of a verifiable historical event, the *resurrection of Jesus*.

In short, the lives and the deaths of James, Peter and Paul are credible circumstantial evidence for the historicity of the resurrection of Jesus, consistent with the more direct evidence above.

The changed attitudes of the early Jewish disciples

The existence and growth of the sect of the Nazarenes

The earliest disciples continued to live as observant Jews, attending the synagogues on the sabbath and the temple at the prescribed hours of prayer (Acts 3:1; 10:3). At the same time, however, they met separately in houses in Jerusalem on the first day of the week and were given the name 'sect of the Nazarenes' due to their affiliation with the man from Nazareth (Acts 24:5). Within a short time, disciples in the Antioch branch of the movement were labelled *Christianoi* (Christians) because of their loyalty to the crucified king of the Jews, the *Christos* (the Christ). These disciples, known as *Nazarenes* and *Christians*, took their names from Jesus of *Nazareth*, who was the *Christ*.

In other words, they belonged to a subset within a Judaism that had other groups, such as Pharisees, Saduccees, Essenes and the Fourth Philosophy (revolutionaries). While those groups doubtless had historic founders, their *ideology* distinguished them in the era of Jesus. With the disciples, however, the thing that distinguished them was their overt commitment to the Nazarene who had been crucified as the Christ. Their attachment to him was primarily *personal*, not ideological.

This connection with him, however, was not with a deceased martyr but one whom they proclaimed to be the risen and exalted Lord and to whom they prayed (e.g. Acts 2:36; 3:14–15). Given the Jewish sense of shame associated with crucifixion, the continuance and growth of the sect of the Nazarenes is inferential evidence of the resurrection of Jesus from the dead.

Group inclusion 'in Christ'

Quite soon apostolic writers were referring to the Christians everywhere, as well as in local congregations, as being 'in Christ'. True, the term is also used of an individual believer being a man or woman 'in Christ'. But what I am thinking of here are the numerous examples in the writings of the New Testament where we find a sense of corporate inclusion under the lordship of Christ. We think, for example, of Paul's use of *temple* and *body* metaphors, and of John's account of believers 'abiding in' Christ as 'branches' in the 'true vine' (1 Cor. 3:16; 12:27; John 15:4).

The point is that this sense of inclusiveness in Christ corresponded with, but exceeded, the sense the Israelites had of being the one covenant people of the Lord, where, for example, they were also called by such corporate terms as the Lord's *vine*, *bride* and *servant* (Ps. 80:8–14; Jer. 3:14; Isa. 49:3).

Since these monotheistic Jewish Christian writers saw Christ relating to his corporate people in ways corresponding to God's relationship corporately with Israel, we must conclude that these writers believed Christ to be an exalted figure, thus presupposing his resurrection.

Continuity

Here I think of radical examples of Jesus' teaching beyond dispute historically, which continued into the post-resurrection church.

One, as we have seen, was his reference to God in the vernacular Aramaic *abba* (father), which we see embedded in the Greek text of several of Paul's letters, where this familial approach to God was evidently commonplace among Greek-speaking disciples in distant provinces. The weight of scholarly opinion is that such a close and personal way of speaking to the Almighty as *abba* was almost unheard of in Jewish piety.

Clearly, though, Jesus' *Abba*, Father, became the *Abba*, Father, of non-Jewish believers in Galatia and Rome.

Another example was Jesus' definitive way of declaring *amēn* as the prefix to his weighty teachings. Jesus' employment of the prefixed *amēn* is without parallel among the rabbis and had the effect of declaring a truth of God as by a solemn oath, implying that God himself was endorsing this teaching. Without further ado or explanation Paul merely informs the Corinthians that Christ himself is the 'yes' to all God's promises in the Scriptures and for this reason believers utter the *amēn* to God through him (2 Cor. 1:20). Again, we observe the seamless continuity between the words of the pre-crucifixion Jesus and the practices of post-crucifixion believers.

A final example is Jesus' astonishing and calculated call of *twelve* disciples, with Jesus himself as their head. Here, as mentioned earlier, we see his implicit messianic claim, as one who was at that very time restoring the twelve tribes to Israel. Without interruption we notice that the earliest church determined to have twelve apostles in continuity to those twelve disciples (Acts 1:12–26).

Each of these examples of continuity presupposes the reality of the resurrection. Mindful of these and similar phenomena, C. F. D. Moule asks, 'If the coming into existence of the Nazarenes . . . rips a great hole in history, a hole the size and shape of the Resurrection, what does the secular historian propose to stop it up with?'[7]

Moule raises another question about how to account historically for the startlingly novel character of the texts of the New Testament. The answer, he says, 'seems to be a most powerful and original mind [Jesus], and a tremendous confirmatory event [his resurrection]'.[8] In short, it was not the resurrection alone, critical as that was, but also the weightiness of the 'powerful and original mind' of the pre-resurrection Jesus that explain the novelty.

Other explanations

Opponents have offered a number of alternative explanations to the New Testament's testimony that Jesus was raised from the dead.

A hoax

History has witnessed many spectacular hoaxes, with some remaining unexploded for considerable periods. Not until 1953, for example, was Charles Dawson's 1912 'Piltdown Man' finally revealed to be the remains of a very modern ape. And in 1994 it was finally revealed that the 1930s photo of the head of the Loch Ness 'monster', which became known worldwide, was actually a device made to deceive.

As I have argued, however, the resurrection of Jesus was unexpected. Jews were then expecting resurrection, but it would happen at the *end* of history and would involve *every* person who had ever died. The scepticism of Thomas to resurrection reports was probably a typical reaction. To assert that *one* person had been raised permanently and bodily *that* day was unexpected.

Likewise, to the Greeks of the period, who believed in the soul's immortality, the declaration that a man had been resurrected was not credible (Acts 17:32).

In short, the hoax explanation assumes ready acceptance of what is proposed, but this was not the case with Jews or Greeks.

Another man was crucified

The Qur'an holds that Jesus was a prophet. Since God would not allow his prophet to be treated that way, another man was crucified in Jesus' place. It states, 'They did not kill [Jesus] nor did they crucify him but they thought they did . . . it was sheer conjecture' (*Sura* 4.156).[9]

This goes against the evidence. It was precisely because Jesus was a public figure in Jerusalem that the temple authorities wanted him out of the way. Thousands of Jewish pilgrims congregated in Jerusalem at Passover. Events had shown that the tiniest spark could ignite riot and tumult in so volatile a situation.

Although Jesus was arrested at night, tried before a hastily convened Sanhedrin and then brought to Pilate in the early hours of the morning, the execution was highly public. Jesus, with two revolutionary activists, was crucified close to the walls of Jerusalem, near a well-used thoroughfare (John 19:20; Mark 15:29).

The very point of crucifixion was to humiliate the criminal *publicly* so as to deter others from such rash behaviour.

There is every indication that it was Jesus who was crucified. Those who mocked him identified him as he hung on the cross, 'He saved others . . .' (Mark 15:31). Roman soldiers were present, guarding the crucified men

Jesus was crucified, not another.

Jesus did not actually die on the cross

The 'swoon' theory was argued in the early 1800s by German scholars Venturini and Paulus and more recently by the British scholar Duncan Derrett.[10] Jesus became unconscious on the cross, but revived in the tomb.

This theory ignores Roman practice. The Jewish historian Josephus records many instances of Roman crucifixion in Palestine. Not only was crucifixion itself violent in the extreme; it was preceded and accompanied by brutal torture. Roman soldiers took advantage of the vulnerability of the victims. Taken together, the scourging and the nailing up of the victim represented an overwhelming assault on the human frame that left the person critically weakened. Those not already dead would have died upon removal from the cross.

Religious art has given a false impression of the man on the cross as motionless and quietly dignified. But the reality would have been different. Death came by asphyxiation. The downward weight of the body constricted breathing, so that the impaled constantly sought to writhe upwards to expand the lungs. The crucified used their feet and legs to lever themselves up so as to breathe.

If, however, the executioners broke the legs, the victims had no leverage and thus could not breathe: death followed quickly.

This is precisely what the Roman soldiers began to do late on that Friday afternoon. Bodies left impaled on the sabbath during Passover brought defilement to the land. When the Jews requested that the three men be killed so as to permit burial before the onset of the sabbath, the Roman soldiers began to break the legs of the victims. When they came to Jesus, however, they found he was already dead.

One of the execution squad thrust a spear into Jesus, to gauge whether he was in fact dead, as he appeared to be. The sudden flow of blood and water was evidence of the reality of the death. Although the dead do not bleed, the blood often remains liquid in the arteries for some hours following asphyxial deaths. Depending on the organs or the blood vessels pierced, for example the inferior *vena cava*, water and serum could indeed issue from someone recently deceased, especially if crucified vertically. The Roman soldiers were trained and experienced at their work.

John, author of the Fourth Gospel, was present when Jesus breathed his last breath. He gives eyewitness testimony that Jesus was truly dead (John 21:24; 19:35).

The body of Jesus remained on the cross until the centurion of the execution squad had come to the prefect, Pontius Pilate, and convinced him Jesus was dead (Mark 15:43–45). The prefect released the body for burial only upon the centurion's assurances that Jesus was, indeed, dead. This was no mere formality in the case of Jesus. The brevity of the time Jesus had been crucified led Pilate to press the question whether or not he was dead. But the answers of the centurion convinced him.

All the evidence points to Jesus' death on the Friday afternoon.

The body was removed from the tomb

The reason the tomb was empty, it is suggested, is that someone removed the corpse between the time of the burial late on the Friday afternoon and the arrival of the women early on the Sunday morning.

Who might have done this and why?

Neither Jews nor Romans would have wanted the body to be other than in the tomb, as powerful evidence that the influential messianic pretender was indeed dead. Such was to be the fate of those who create public disturbance against the might of Rome and her emperor! The Jews and the Romans could point to both the place where he was crucified and the place where he was buried. The bones of Jesus in the tomb in which he was buried would stand as an irrefutable denial of the claims he had made and the hopes invested in him.

In any case, had either Jew or Roman taken the body, they would immediately have produced it when the disciples began to proclaim that Jesus was raised alive. It was widely believed at the time that the *disciples* had taken the body. But Matthew states that the temple authorities bribed the Roman soldiers to say this (Matt. 28:11–15). Matthew's rebuttal of the widespread belief among the Jews that the disciples had taken the body is evidence that the tomb in which Jesus had been buried did not contain his body. Throughout the next two centuries the Jewish counterclaim was that the disciples had taken the body (see Justin Martyr, *Dialogue with Trypho* 108; and Tertullian, *The Shows* 30).

The disciples had come to Jerusalem armed (Luke 22:49–50; John 19:10; cf. Luke 19:11), probably expecting a messianic show-down (Acts 1:6; cf. Luke 24:21). They did not expect Jesus to be raised, because they did not expect him to be killed. By definition the Messiah was a victor and they had come with him to share in the spoils of his apocalyptic triumph. On the way to Jerusalem James and John wanted to have places of power when he entered into his glory (Mark 10:35–37). Jesus' words about his death and resurrection, as they travelled to Jerusalem, were simply not under-stood (Mark 9:10; 10:32). The report of the women that the tomb was empty and that Jesus' promise that he would be raised the third day had been fulfilled was greeted by the disciples with disbe-lief as an idle tale (Luke 24:11).

The suggestion, then, that these deeply disappointed men, steeped in an apocalyptic world view, suddenly thought of stealing the body and saying that Jesus, as an individual, had been raised from the dead before the onset of the end of the world is highly improbable.

The women returned to the wrong tomb

This explanation states that the women made the simplest mistake. They returned to the wrong tomb, found it empty and declared that the Lord had risen.[11]

By the time Jesus had died it was middle to late afternoon; a new day, the sabbath, would soon begin. With the rapid approach of the Passover sabbath, Jesus had to be taken from the cross and interred, otherwise the land would be defiled (Deut. 21:23; John 19:31, 42).

The records show that Joseph of Arimathea, a member of the Sanhedrin, made his as yet unused tomb available for the burial of Jesus (Matt. 27:60). From the records it is clear that Joseph's tomb was close to Golgotha, the site of the crucifixion (John 19:40, 42). Golgotha itself was close to the walls of Jerusalem; the *titulus* (inscription attached to Jesus' cross) could be read from the city wall (John 19:20). In other words, the tomb was readily locatable, being (1) close to Jesus' cross, which was close to the city walls, and (2) doubtless a substantial tomb, belonging to one of the most prominent members of the community.

Each Gospel tells us that the tomb to which the women came and that they found to be empty belonged to a man of high profile with whom the story could be readily checked.

Moreover, the Gospels indicate that the women sat opposite the tomb; they saw 'where' and 'how' the burial occurred (Matt. 27:61; Mark 15:47; Luke 23:55). The 'mistaken tomb' explanation is improbable and goes against the evidence given for the burial of Jesus.

But disciples also came to the tomb, on the report of the women (Luke 24:24). John, author of the Fourth Gospel, was one of those who came to the tomb. He testified as an eyewitness that only Jesus' burial cloths were found in the tomb (John 20:5–8). The presence of burial cloths confirms that the women had, indeed, come to the right place. Clearly, they had come to the tomb in which Jesus had recently been buried.

The resurrection stories are legendary

It is well established that legends take many years, in fact decades and centuries, to develop.

But *the first day of the week* tradition arose from the women who went to the tomb. It became fixed immediately, as the significant day of the week, because from the beginning the disciples began to meet on that day, the first day of the week to commemorate the Lord's resurrection (John 20:26; cf. Acts 20:7; 1 Cor. 16:2).

The other tradition, that Christ was raised on the *third day*, also became critical in early Christianity. It arose in Jerusalem soon after the resurrection and became embedded in the tradition Paul 'received' (1 Cor. 15:3–8).

These markers (*the first day of the week* and the *on the third day* traditions) arose immediately after the resurrection of Jesus and for no other reason, except to describe the reality of what had happened. On *the first day of the week* (Sunday) the tomb was empty because *on the third day* after his crucifixion (Sunday) Jesus had been raised from the dead.

The earliness and sober concreteness of these traditions about the resurrection is quite different from the vague and frequently bizarre notions associated with the evolution of legends.

The resurrection originated in the Osiris myth

Some people argue that the Egyptian myth of Isis and Osiris was the real source of the New Testament proclamation of the resurrection of Jesus. The ancient Egyptian myth of Isis and Osiris, in Hellenized form, became a popular cult around the Mediterranean world in the centuries after Alexander's conquest of Egypt in the fourth century BC.

According to the myth, Osiris, a pharaoh, was murdered and mutilated by his brother, Set. Isis, Osiris' sister and wife, collected and buried his remains and caused him to be reanimated as the god of the dead. Thus Osiris reigns over the underworld as a mummy; his 'new life' is a replica of earthly life.

The association of Jesus with Osiris was fashionable in the early twentieth century, largely through the influence of James Frazer's *The Golden Bough*, published in 1906. The German scholar Rudolph Bultmann advocated a version of the dying and rising god as the explanation of the resurrection of Jesus. Bultmann's supposed parallels, however, all postdate the New Testament by several hundred years.

Few today pursue this line of thought.

We should note that (1) the grotesque story of Isis and Osiris is quite unlike the account of the resurrection of Jesus; (2) as devout Jews, and therefore monotheists, the disciples would have had no part in an idolatrous Gentile cult or its beliefs; (3) the account of Jesus gives people, time and place specifics that, by their nature, are absent from myths, which are ahistorical; (4) the formal credo about the resurrection of Jesus had been established within so brief a period as two or three years of the event; and (5) Jesus is not a reanimated god over the nether regions; rather, he is alive for evermore, the Lord both of the dead and the living (Rev. 1:18; Rom. 14:9).

Summary

When carefully considered, my conclusion is that these and related theories are unconvincing. Strikingly, those who reject the resurrection of Jesus have not settled on one major objection to the historicity of the resurrection.

Evaluation of the evidence

The analysis of the resurrection belongs to disciplines that evaluate *evidence*, in particular those of the historian and lawyer. Over the years many noted scientists and historians have argued for the resurrection of Jesus based on evidence.

Francis Collins, Head of the Human Genome Project and former atheist, in his book *The Language of God* describes how his pride and sinfulness prevented him from knowing God. However, the weight of historical evidence convinced him of the truth of the crucifixion and resurrection of Jesus and so he became a Christian believer.[12]

William Lane Craig, historian and philosopher, comments:

> I argue that four established facts (Jesus' burial, the empty tomb, postmortem appearances, and the origin of the Christian way) provide adequate inductive grounds for inferring Jesus' resurrection [and that] it is very difficult to deny that the resurrection of Jesus is the best explanation of these four facts. Thus there are good historical grounds for affirming that Jesus rose from the dead.[13]

The discipline of legal prosecution closely resembles that of the historian. Both must weigh and evaluate evidence as a basis for arriving at a reasonable conclusion. The jurist, Sir Edward Clarke, comments that

> The evidence for [the events of the first Easter Day] is conclusive, and over and over again in the High Court I have secured the verdict on evidence not nearly so compelling . . . a truthful witness is always artless and disdains effect. The Gospel evidence for the resurrection is of this class and, as a lawyer, I accept it unreservedly as the testimony of truthful men to facts they were able to substantiate.[14]

Reduced to basics, the alternatives are either (1) that one accepts the evidence as true, or (2) concludes that the first Christians were mistaken or that they perpetrated an elaborate fraud. But for many, the quality of the evidence and the moral tone of the literature where it occurs leads them to conclude that Jesus, having been crucified, was after three days raised from the dead on the first day of Passover week.

Significance of the resurrection

The case I have been putting is that the worship of Jesus as 'Lord' by the early Christians (a fact) is entirely consistent with his pre-resurrection persona as Messiah, Son of God and Son of Man. The alternative, that Jesus was *only* a prophet or rabbi, leaves unexplained the immediate worship of him post-resurrection. Rather, his supranatural identity, powerful mission and miracles find a logical continuity after his death as one proclaimed and venerated as the exalted Lord.

What was the role of the resurrection in this? In my view the resurrection confirmed Jesus' pre-resurrection identity and mission as Messiah. It did not, however, make Jesus into someone he had not been beforehand.

15. MESSIAH IN THE ORAL TRADITION

We preach Messiah crucified . . .
(Paul, 1 Cor. 1:23)

The earliest *written* Gospel, attributed to Mark shortly after the New Testament era, identifies itself in its opening words as just that, a *Gospel*. Mark's Gospel is a kind of biography, but one he wrote to be *read aloud* to gathered groups. He planned it to be, in effect, the equivalent of a modern audiotape. At one point he gives the public reader directions about the need to explain what he has written (Mark 13:14).

Jesus (as reported by Mark) expected the *overall message* of this written Gospel to be *verbally* 'proclaimed to *all* the nations' and 'in the *whole* world' (Mark 13:10; 14:9; both my tr.). At the same time, however, Jesus said that the *component stories* in his gospel were to be 'told' everywhere. In other words, 'gospel' was both (1) an oral message about Jesus, to be 'preached' (to unbelievers), and (2) a written biography about Jesus, to be 'read aloud', containing stories to be 'told'. Either way, it was a message to be *heard* that called for a response of faith in and obedience to the Messiah.

'Gospel' in 1 Corinthians 15

From Paul's letters, the earliest written texts in the New Testament, it is clear that *summarized* versions of a Jesus 'biography' already existed in *oral* form, predating Mark's written form. Paul quotes a section of that gospel-biography (the items as of 'first importance' for the current pastoral concerns in Corinth) to remind the believers in Corinth of his initial *gospel preaching* that brought their church into existence circa AD 50:

> Now I would remind you, brethren,
> in what terms I *preached* to you the *gospel* . . .
> For I delivered to you as of first importance what I also received,
>> that *Christ* died for our sins in accordance with the scriptures,
>> that he was buried,
>> that he was raised on the third day in accordance with the
>>> scriptures, and
>> that he appeared to Cephas,
>>> then to the twelve.
>>> Then he appeared to more than five hundred brethren
>>>> at one time . . .
>>> Then he appeared to James,
>>> then to all the apostles.
>
> (1 Cor. 15:1–7)

This early oral recitation was focused on the Messiah, his death for sins in fulfilment of Scripture, his burial, his resurrection on the third day in fulfilment of Scripture and his appearances alive to numerous witnesses (see above, chapter 11).

This summarized gospel-biography of the latter (Jerusalem) end of the Messiah's lifespan is focused on his bodily resurrection. This was because the resurrection of the body was the contentious issue in Corinth Paul needed to address in this chapter ('Now if Christ is preached as raised from the dead, how can some of you say that there is no resurrection of the dead?'; 15:12). To buttress his arguments Paul reminds them that apostles (including he himself and the Jerusalem leaders Peter and James) *proclaim* exactly the same Messiah-based gospel he does (1 Cor. 15:11):

> Whether then it was *I or they* [the Jerusalem apostles],
> so *we*
>> preach, and
> so you [Corinthians] believed.
> (1 Cor. 15:11)

So between the Jerusalem-based apostles and Paul there was a commonly agreed *oral*, summarized gospel-biography about the Messiah crucified but resurrected.

Furthermore, we must note two other and related aspects about this *verbal* gospel-biography. First, Paul did not formulate it, but rather 'received' it. Secondly, Paul 'received' it early, in the shadow of the historical Christ, either from the apostles Peter and James in Jerusalem circa 36, or more probably from the disciples in Damascus circa 34, who in turn had earlier 'received' it from the Jerusalem apostles.

Here we note rabbinical overtones from the ex-Pharisee. As Paul 'received' the 'gospel' 'delivered' to him, so he 'delivered' it to the Corinthians who likewise 'received' it from him. The point to emphasize is that this biographical summary arose from the apostolic leaders in Jerusalem: Paul merely 'delivered' to others the words that came originally *from the Jerusalem leaders.*

The ultimate source of this commonly agreed apostolic gospel was Peter, the first apostolic leader in Jerusalem (Gal. 2:7–8).

1 Corinthians 15:3–5 and Acts 10:40–41, 43

There are strikingly similar elements between the latter parts of Peter's message (the 'Jerusalem' narrative) to Cornelius in Caesarea Maritima and Paul's cited gospel in 1 Corinthians 15:3–5. See the table below.

In these two passages we see the convergence of ideas but also close verbal parallels. Both passages teach the following:

• The vicarious death of 'the Messiah' for sins.
• Thereby fulfilling the prophetic Scriptures.

- God raised the Messiah 'on the third day', fulfilling the prophetic Scriptures.
- He appeared alive to many living witnesses.

1 Corinthians 15:3–5	Acts 10:40–41, 43 (Peter is the speaker)
Christ *died for our sins in accordance with the scriptures.*	To him *all the prophets* bear witness that every one who believes in him receives *forgiveness of sins through his name.*
He was *raised* [by God] on the *third day.*	God *raised* him on the *third day.*
He appeared to *Cephas* . . . the Twelve . . . etc.	God made him manifest . . . to *us* . . . witnesses.

So striking are these common ideas and words that some theory of dependence is to be inferred. The most probable explanation is that a prior Peter-tradition was the basis of the tradition Paul himself had 'received', which he then 'delivered' to the churches of his mission, as in Corinth.

So we can make the following observation: Paul's verbal gospel-biography, which he stated as a reminder for specific pastoral reasons in Corinth, coincides closely with the same 'Jerusalem' part of Peter's verbal gospel (Acts 10:36). Accordingly, we can reasonably argue that had Paul needed to, he could have listed other elements of Peter's summarized verbal gospel-biography, elements that began with John the Baptist and continued with Jesus' own preaching and healing in Galilee. In other words, I propose that Paul could have cited a biographical summary that broadly corresponded with Peter's earlier 'Galilee' section, as in Acts 10:36–39a.

This, indeed, is precisely what we find in the single biographical summary attributed to Paul in the book of Acts (13:23–31), as discussed below.

What, then, are we to conclude from this evidence in 1 Corinthians 15:3–5 and Acts 10:40–41, 43? Put simply, it means that soon after the first Easter the Jerusalem apostles formulated a verbal gospel-biography for preaching purposes. Shortly afterwards, Paul 'received' this message, which in turn he 'delivered' to the churches of his Gentile mission; hence his claim that he and the Jerusalem apostles Cephas and James proclaimed the same gospel.

Subsequently, Mark expanded the original verbal gospel as a comprehensive *written* gospel-biography whose twin purposes were (1) for reading to assembled disciples, but (2) also as the basis of gospel stories to be 'told' in the churches in 'all the nations' in 'the whole world' (Mark 13:10; 14:9). As discussed in a previous chapter, the source of Mark's Gospel was the eyewitness and leading disciple Peter. Mark wrote his Gospel based on his recollections of his verbal translations of Peter's preaching.

Paul in Antioch in Pisidia (Acts 13:16–41)

In circa 47 Paul and Barnabas came to Antioch in Pisidia (Yalvaç in modern Turkey), where Paul, the trained Pharisee and biblical scholar, was invited to preach in the synagogue. In this, Paul's only recorded synagogue sermon, he provides extensive biographical information about John the Baptist and what happened to Jesus in Jerusalem. It is of utmost importance that we recognize that Paul identifies his summarized *oral* Jesus-biography as 'gospel' (Acts 13:32).[1]

But how confident are we that we are hearing the voice of Paul, and not that of the author of the Acts of the Apostles? The historian Thucydides set a high standard for the speeches he reports in his chronicle of the Peloponnesian Wars (fifth century BC). Thucydides acknowledges that he 'put into the mouth of each speaker the sentiments proper to the occasion . . . while at the same time . . . to give the general purport of *what was actually said*' (*History of the Peloponnesian War* 1.22.1).[2] In my opinion Luke was at least as careful in his summaries of speeches as was Thucydides, the doyen of Greek historians.

There is good reason to believe that this is a genuine sermon by Paul. In particular, there are elements in the summary of it that point to the conventions of a typical synagogue homily.[3] In other words, of all the sermons recorded in the book of Acts this is the one most like a synagogue exposition, and it came from the lips of Paul, a well-qualified synagogue teacher known to us in the New

Testament. The author of Acts, Luke, was a Gentile and unlikely to have been able to replicate the elements of a synagogue sermon, as we find them in Acts 13 (Col. 4:11, 14).

The Sermons of Peter (Acts 10:34–43) and Paul (Acts 13:16–41)

Paul's gospel-sermon at Antioch in Pisidia circa 47 is much longer than Peter's a decade earlier at Caesarea Maritima. Most probably this is due to Luke's greater access to Paul and his preaching than to Peter's ministry. Paul was Luke's close friend, whereas Peter may have been only an acquaintance.

There are other differences. Unlike Peter's sermon at Caesarea, Paul asserts that Jesus is the 'seed of David' who, unlike his famous forebear, did not see corruption following death. As well, Peter offers no comment about the culpability of the rulers in Jerusalem for the death of Christ, whereas Paul is critical of their rejection of Jesus. Further, Peter expands on Jesus' ministry in Galilee, the 'country of the Jews' (Acts 10:38; rural Galilee, not urban Jerusalem), whereas Paul makes no reference to Jesus' ministry in Galilee, though he does mention 'those who came up with him from Galilee to Jerusalem' (Acts 13:31). Despite differences in length and content the two summarized sermons have a common biographical thread. See the table below (p. 170).

These sermons are different in tone and setting, yet follow the same broad sequence, beginning with John the Baptist and ending with the death, resurrection and appearances of the Risen One in Jerusalem.

Oral gospel and written Gospel

Let me make seven observations about 'gospel':

1. The word 'gospel' (as noun or verb) is used to describe the summarized *verbal* biographies of Jesus, as spoken by both Peter and Paul (Acts 10:36; 13:32).

2. This oral gospel originated early in Jerusalem and was formulated by the apostles, under the leadership of Peter.

3. Soon afterwards Paul 'received' this gospel summary, either in Damascus or Jerusalem.

4. This summarized gospel-biography has a biographical thread, that begins with John's preaching of baptism, followed by Jesus' ministry in Galilee, and ends with his death, resurrection and risen appearances in Jerusalem.

5. This gospel-biography about the Messiah's coming, death and resurrection was in fulfilment of Old Testament prophecy.

6. The word 'gospel' appears as the *title* of the earliest *written* 'Gospel'.

7. The earliest written Gospel (Mark's) follows exactly the same sequence as the oral gospel of Peter and Paul.

Peter (Acts 10)	*Paul (Acts 13)*
John's preaching of baptism	John preached a baptism of repentance
	Jesus, 'seed' of David (Messiah)
Jesus the *Messiah*, who is Lord of all, preached and healed in Galilee	
Peter a witness in Galilee and Judea	
The Jews in Jerusalem put him to death	Jerusalemites and rulers secured his death at Pilate's hands
	They buried him in a tomb
God raised him on the third day	God raised him from the dead
God made him manifest to chosen witnesses	He appeared to those who came up from Galilee for many days
These he commanded to preach to the people	These were now witnesses to the people.

Historically, the *oral* gospel of the Messiah predated the *written* Gospel of Mark and dictated its broad sequence. Yet, as noted above, the author of the written Gospel (based on Christ's mandate) expected the *oral* version of his written text to be read to congregations and for the constituent stories in the Gospel to be told throughout the world.

Conclusion: the Messiah in proclamation and text

The early oral biography of the Messiah that the apostles formulated in Jerusalem after the resurrection and that was expanded as the written Gospel is evidence of the impact of the pre-resurrection Jesus on his original disciples.

This was vital biographical information about the life, death and resurrection of the Messiah, whom they worshipped as 'Lord of all'. The Gospels firmly rooted the Messiah of Israel in the events of history and the soil of Palestine (in the era of the emperor Tiberius). The worship of a man as 'Lord' could very easily have developed as a species of ahistorical myths, as indeed happened in Gnostic circles in the centuries following. The *oral* gospel (later overtaken and superseded by the *written* Gospel), dotted with historical and geographical references, saved the early Christians from thinking of Christ as a world-denying mythical redeemer.

When Mark came to write what was to be the earliest written Gospel circa 70, he was merely extending and formalizing the verbal gospelling of the previous forty or so years. The difference was merely one of degree and format. The essential message was the same. In any case, the Gospel that came to be written was also written for a verbal purpose, for the stories about Jesus to be *read aloud* in assembled church meetings.

So successful was Mark's achievement that Matthew and Luke took his Gospel as authoritative and true, and merely shortened it at various points to incorporate other genuine source material (Q, L, M).

We may express it like this. Matthew and Luke were expanded versions of Mark; Mark was a written version of the oral gospel; the main outlines of the oral gospel were established in Jerusalem soon after the resurrection by the apostles led by Peter.

John, however, while probably knowing of Mark's existence (but not his precise contents) and agreeing with his overall narrative sequence expresses his Gospel in his own idiosyncratic format and idiom. Nonetheless, it is almost certain that John's Gospel began as a series of oral narrations about Jesus that the author finally completed as almost identical to the written Gospel as we have it today. This Gospel portrays Palestinian religious culture in the years before the Roman invasion in AD 66. There is no reason that the Gospel of John should be dated later than the sixties or seventies. While written originally in Palestine, possibly John 'issued' it some years later with minor changes in Ephesus in Roman Asia. Its narrative setting, however, is emphatically Palestinian, not Anatolian. Its cultural world is thus not Ephesus but Jerusalem.

16. MESSIAH'S CHURCHES

The rise of early Christianity is the story of the early preaching of the gospel of the Messiah and the consequent creation of the various churches. The history of the rise of the movement is the history of the proliferation of the churches, first in Palestine and from there throughout the Roman provinces that ringed the Mediterranean.

While the New Testament calls them 'churches', we must be careful not to imagine them to be like churches today, nor even as those of late antiquity. On the contrary, and of great importance, they were *groups of people* who met in private homes.

Furthermore, as in the letter of James (2:2; cf. 5:14), the original gatherings of Jewish disciples were probably called 'synagogues'. The word 'church' was probably chosen later to distinguish the Messiah-followers from mainline synagogue attendees, on the one hand, and Gentile temple worshippers, on the other hand.

The choice of the term 'church' (Greek, *ekklēsia*) was inspired. The word occurred in the Greek Old Testament (the Septuagint) for the great gatherings of God's people (e.g. Deut. 23:21; 1 Chr. 28:8). But it was also commonly used in the Greek-speaking world for an everyday 'meeting' or 'assembly', including for local political associations. Thus 'church' established continuity with the history of the covenant people (from whom Christians were the rightful successors), while avoiding words like *thiasos* that would connect them with pagan religions.[1] In the Gentile world, outsiders would have struggled to understand these 'Christians', since they did not seem to fit into any known category, whether religious, cultural or political.

The proliferation of churches

The first church: Jerusalem AD 33

The first church, although it was not so called, was the small band of twelve Galilean disciples (with others) whom Jesus gathered and taught. After the resurrection, they became the foundation apostles of the church in Jerusalem, whose leaders were Peter and John. Quite soon a group of Greek-speaking Jews ('Hellenists') attached themselves to the Galileans ('Hebrews'). So for a brief period the church in Jerusalem was composed of Jews who were more specifically 'Hebrews' (first language Aramaic) and Jews who were 'Hellenists' (first language Greek), under the leadership of Peter and the apostles.

Churches in Judea, Samaria and Galilee circa 35

A young Pharisee, Saul of Tarsus, led an attack on the whole (mixed) church in Jerusalem on account of the Hellenist Stephen's attack on the role of the temple in the purposes of God. Apart from the apostles, the members of the church were scattered throughout the three regions of Israel: Judea (Gal. 1:22; 1 Thess. 2:14), Samaria and Galilee. Like scattered seeds these dispersed disciples established Messiah house churches in Judea, Samaria and Galilee. Peter (and John?) assumed responsibility to look after these scattered churches throughout the three regions of the land of Israel.

Both the book of Acts and Paul's letter to the Galatians indicate the leadership of Peter in the churches in Judea, Samaria and Galilee that had sprung up following Saul's attack on the church in Jerusalem:

> So the church throughout all Judea and Galilee and Samaria
> had peace and was built up;
> and walking in the fear of the Lord and in the comfort of the Holy
>   Spirit
> it was multiplied.
> Now as *Peter* went here and there among them all . . .
> (Acts 9:31–32)

> *Peter* had been entrusted with the gospel to the circumcised . . . [God] worked through Peter for the mission to the circumcised . . . (Gal. 2:8–9)

It is impossible to exaggerate the importance of Peter in these earliest years of Christian history in Israel. Jesus anticipated that Peter would become a future leader and for that reason called him the 'rock'.

Hellenist churches in Judea circa 35–55

Paul's attack effectively drove many Hellenist disciples permanently from Jerusalem. Some sought refuge in Damascus, where, ironically, the now-converted Paul joined their ranks!

However, the Hellenist leader Philip (later known as 'the evangelist') remained in Israel, establishing a missionary base in Caesarea from which he established a network of churches on the coastal plain, including in Ptolemais, Sidon and Tyre (Acts 21:7; 27:3, 7).

Other Hellenists remained in and around Jerusalem, probably forming the rump of the persecuted church addressed in the letter to the Hebrews.[2]

Syria and Cilicia circa 35–45

But other Hellenists travelled north beyond the borders of Israel to the great cosmopolitan metropolis Antioch, capital of Syria.

Soon these Hellenists established the first church to have Gentile as well as Jewish members. It was here that the disciples of the Lord were for the first time called 'Messiahmen' ('Christians').

Meanwhile, Paul returned from Damascus to Jerusalem and from there (after a period) to his birthplace, Tarsus, in the region of Cilicia. After some years, churches in the province of Syria and Cilicia had been established through the missionary activities of Paul (Acts 15:23, 41).

Paul's westward mission to the Gentiles circa 47–57

In circa 47 Barnabas and Paul, leaders of the church in Antioch received the agreement of the Jerusalem church (James, Peter and John) to go more intentionally to the Gentiles. During the following year or so they travelled to Cyprus, Pisidia and Lycaonia (central Turkey) making converts and establishing churches. Subsequently, Barnabas and his younger cousin John Mark separated from Paul and revisited Cyprus for further mission work and, we assume, the creation of churches, though evidence is lacking.

Paul took another associate, Silvanus, from Jerusalem and re-visited the churches in Syria-Cilicia, Lycaonia and Pisidia, being joined by his younger co-worker Timothy. They travelled west and north, ultimately arriving at Alexandria Troas (near Troy), where they were joined by Luke, before crossing the northern Aegean to Macedonia. While Luke remained in northern Macedonia (in and around Philippi), Paul, Silvanus and Timothy established churches further south in Macedonia in Philippi, Thessalonica and Beroea.

Paul travelled south to Achaia, where he preached in Athens and Corinth and established a church in Corinth. In time, other churches were established in Achaia, including at Corinth's Aegean port, Cenchreae.

Next Paul returned briefly to Jerusalem and Antioch. Again travelling overland westward he revisited the churches of Lycaonia and Pisidia before arriving in the great city of Ephesus, capital of Roman Asia, where he remained for about three years. During those years his co-worker the evangelist Epaphras created a network of churches in the Lycus Valley (Colossae, Laodicea and

Hierapolis). Meanwhile, a church had been established in Troas (by Luke?).

The house groups in Rome circa 57

Paul's letter to the Roman believers, unlike other letters, is not addressed to a church; that is, a single gathering of disciples. From the final chapter of the letter it appears that believers met in a series of loosely connected house meetings. The beginnings of Christianity in Rome are shrouded in mystery. Perhaps its founders were Roman Jews who had been baptized and instructed by Peter and the apostles in Jerusalem at the feast of Pentecost before returning to Italy. Possibly, these disciples continued to attend the synagogues in Rome as well as Christian meetings. One of Paul's reasons for writing Romans was to create a single church in the Eternal City composed of Jews and Gentiles from these disparate groups.

The churches of Paul's mission

Through his missionary journeys Paul created churches in the Roman provinces of Syria-Cilicia, Cyprus (?), Galatia, Macedonia, Achaia and Asia. This was a massive achievement, probably unparalleled in Christian history, especially since most of this happened in a mere decade (47–57)!

Paul was assisted by many associates, in particular Timothy, Titus, and Paul's faithful travelling companion Luke, who probably wrote his Acts partly as an apologia for his friend Paul.

The churches of James

James's letter is an encyclical to Jewish Christians. Its Greek text and address to 'the twelve tribes in the Dispersion' (Jas 1:1) suggests that James wrote it from Jerusalem to fellow Jewish believers worldwide, whether in Palestine or the diaspora. James's death in AD 62 points to an early date for his letter. Possibly, his letter, as early as the forties, is the earliest written text of the New Testament.

There is reason to believe that Matthew wrote his Gospel for a similar readership as the letter of James; that is, for Greek-speaking Jewish believers in both Palestine and the Diaspora.

The churches of Peter

In the early sixties Peter wrote a circular letter from 'Babylon' (code name for Rome) to scattered believers in the Roman provinces of Pontus, Galatia, Cappadocia, Asia and Bithynia; that is, in the greater part of northern Anatolia. It is not known who established these churches over such a vast area or even certain that Peter had visited them, though his greetings sent from Mark suggests these readers knew (or knew of) Mark (1 Pet. 5:12–13). Probably, the churches addressed were in the more northerly parts of Anatolia as distinct from the more southerly parts of Galatia and Asia that Paul evangelized.

The churches of John

The apostle John migrated to Ephesus sometime after circa 57, when Paul finally left the Aegean region. Early evidence points to John's lengthy sojourn in those parts extending almost to the turn of the century. It appears that in Roman Asia he 'issued' the Gospel he had written earlier in Palestine, as well as his three letters and the Apocalypse. John's influence can be seen in the Apocalypse, his authoritative encyclical to seven churches scattered throughout the central western part of Roman Asia.

Summary

The spread of Christianity in its first fifty years was both rapid and uncoordinated. The movement was blessed in its earliest history for the robust and untiring men who led the various overlapping (sometimes competing) missions. These leaders faced the daunting challenges of the danger of travel by land and sea and of opposition from the Jewish communities as well as outright persecution from the Roman authorities. Yet they pressed on in the face of hardship and martyrdom. The emergence of Christendom three centuries later was the legacy of their labours.

Their primary activity was to proclaim that the Messiah was Jesus, crucified, risen and returning, and to gather believers into faith communities called 'churches'.

Life together in Messiah's meetings

As Jews, Jesus and his disciples attended weekly sabbath synagogue meetings. Important features of synagogue life carried over into the earliest Jewish churches; for example, the routine of weekly meetings (now on Sundays) and the practice of liturgical benedictions, prayers and the public reading of the sacred writings with exposition. Furthermore, the pattern of synagogue government was probably continued in the Christian practice of appointing local elders.

There were aspects of synagogue life the early churches sought to avoid. One was the notorious hypocrisy of many (but not all) Pharisees and the liturgical inflexibility of the synagogue meetings.

Following are some of the differentiating attitudes the leaders sought to inculcate in the common life of the Messiah-groups.

Equality

Stratification according to wealth, status and official position characterized both Jewish and Gentile community life in the era of Jesus. Church leadership, however, was to be functional and, unlike the Jewish priesthood, not hereditary (1 Thess. 5:13). James admonished the rich to care for the poor, and for members generally not to discriminate against the poor (Jas 2:1–13; 5:1–6). Paul taught that 'in Christ' men and women, slaves and free, Jew and Greek were all one (Gal. 3:28), and he railed against 'those who have' acting unfairly against 'those who have not' (1 Cor. 11:17–22).

Affection

The 'holy kiss' both men and women shared was an outward sign of the deep friendship among the believers (e.g. Rom. 16:14; 1 Pet. 5:14). Indeed, they were brothers and sisters, children of the God they called '*Abba*, Father', whose love for each other was to be heartfelt and unhypocritical (Rom. 12:9–11; 1 Pet. 1:22; 2:1; 3:8; 4:8). An others-centred, not self-centred, life was to be the norm (1 Cor. 13).

Practical care of disadvantaged members

The sharing of meals in hospitality and the care of widows and orphans was held out as practical, standard behaviour among believers (Rom. 12:13; Heb. 13:2; Jas 1:27; 1 Pet. 4:9; cf. Acts 6:1).

Fervour

The Messiah's meetings were marked by joyful and enthusiastic fervour. Members spontaneously offered hymns, prophecies, tongues and revelations in the Corinthian meetings. Although this spontaneity may have been greater in Corinth, there are strong hints that it was also part of church life elsewhere (1 Cor. 14:26; cf. Rom. 12:11; 1 Thess. 5:19–20).

Acclamation of Jesus as Lord

The acclamation of Jesus as Lord, the singing of hymns *to* the Lord, and the invocation *Maran atha* meant church gatherings were focused on the risen and exalted Messiah (Rom. 10:9; 1 Cor. 12:3; 16:22; Eph. 5:19).

Heaven anticipated

The writer to the Hebrews taught his readers that in their gatherings they were like priests in a temple of the Lord, spiritually brought into his presence in heaven:

> But you have come
> to Mount Zion
> and to the city of the living God, the heavenly Jerusalem,
> and to innumerable angels in festal gathering,
> and to the assembly of the first-born who are enrolled in heaven,
> and to a judge who is God of all,
> and to the spirits of just men made perfect,
> and to Jesus, the mediator of a new covenant,
> and to the sprinkled blood that speaks more graciously than the blood
> of Abel.
> (Heb. 12:22–24)

The idea that these believers meeting in an ordinary home were priests in a temple of the Lord was widely held in the New Testament era (1 Cor. 3:16; 2 Cor. 6:16; Eph. 2:19–22; 1 Pet. 2:4–5; Rev. 1:6).

Expectation

The Aramaic invocation *Maran atha*, repeated in the Apocalypse (Rev. 22:20), is evidence that the Messiah's churches were waiting expectantly for the return of the Lord.

Spirit-power

The gathered disciples believed that some of their members were enabled to speak a prophetic word from the Lord, so as to give a word of knowledge or wisdom as needed (1 Cor. 12:8; 14:29–32; cf. Acts 13:1–3). Others had been given 'gifts of healings' so that 'works of power' were part of their experience of church life (1 Cor. 12:9–10; Gal. 3:5; Heb. 6:5).

Summary

The churches of the Messiah among the Jews and the Gentiles had many similarities with the synagogues in Palestine and the diaspora, in particular in their emphasis on reading the sacred writings and in some aspects of church government.

At the same time, however, they were freer and more spontaneous in their affections and outpouring of joy and love, with many
examples of Spirit-power evident in their midst. In these and other
distinguishing matters, they embodied the loving care of the
Messiah Jesus to his disciples in Galilee and Judea and, moreover,
in the exercise of 'gifts' they gave expression to the indwelling
Spirit who had come to them soon after their Lord's exaltation.

Activities in the churches

The New Testament letters and the book of Acts give us windows
into the activities that typically occurred in the Messiah's churches.

Reading and teaching the sacred writings

The members of the churches continued the synagogue practice
of reading from the sacred writings (1 Tim. 4:13). From very early
times, the words and deeds of the Messiah were recorded in
shorter texts; for example, the 'Jerusalem' narrative of what would
later be the concluding part of the Gospel of Mark (chs. 11–16)
and other texts that would later be woven into the Gospels of
Matthew and Luke (Q, L and M; Luke 1:1–4). Evidently, the public
reading of texts and teaching thereon were a major part of church
gatherings from early times (Mark 13:14; Col. 4:16; Rev. 1:3; 22:18).
In societies where literacy was limited, the role of the lector/
reader was important.

Lord's Supper

Because of aberrations Paul had to remind the Corinthians of the
directions the Lord Jesus had given at the Last Supper about the
thanksgiving meal he instituted to commemorate his death (1 Cor.
11:17–22). Paul had 'received' these directions from those who were
'in Christ' before him (most probably at Damascus or Jerusalem).

The wording of Paul's reminder pointed believers *back* historically to the saving death of the Messiah 'on the night he was
betrayed', but also *up* in adoration of the One who was Lord. It

was the *Lord's* Supper, the 'table of the *Lord*', and the 'cup of the *Lord*' (1 Cor. 11:20; 11:27; 10:21). Also, they heard the Lord's words and ate and drank in anticipation of his return, perhaps in that setting calling out *Maran atha.*

Since church gatherings were in homes, it was natural to conduct the thanksgiving meal within a general meal. Most probably the owner of the house would offer the thanksgiving prayer. After Christians began meeting in separate church buildings (late in the second century), the Lord's Supper tended to become a separated ritual act led by a presbyter.

Baptism

People became members of Messiah's churches by being baptized 'in the name of the Lord Jesus' (Acts 8:16; cf. 2:38; 10:48). They were said to have been 'baptized into Christ [Messiah]', where the historical events of his death, burial and resurrection were re-enacted as the convert went down into and came up from the water (Rom. 6:3).

Beforehand, however, there was careful instruction about Christ, salvation and the essentials of Christian behaviour (Rom. 6:17). The role of catechizing new converts became important in the churches (Gal. 6:6; cf. Luke 1:4).

Prophesying

Spirit-led prophesying was an important activity in the Messiah's churches. This 'gift' was widely practised in the churches, including by women (Acts 21:9; 1 Cor. 11:5; Rev. 2:20). 'Prophesying' seems to have involved a Scripture-based 'revelation' intended to impart practical 'wisdom', 'knowledge', 'instruction', 'comfort' or 'encouragement' (1 Cor. 12:7–11; 13:2; 14:3, 24, 29). Paul strongly encouraged 'prophesying' because it 'built up' the church and converted visiting unbelievers.

Praying

Some of the liturgical practices of the synagogues were adapted for use in the churches, notably the *benediction* or blessing of God.

Other set forms were developed by the believers; for example, the *invocation* of the name of the Lord, the appeal to *Abba*, the *thanksgiving*, *grace* and *doxology*.

Equally, however, the churches gave expression to spontaneous outbursts of faith and hope and the free exercise of 'gifts'. These, together with relatively fixed forms of words at baptism and the thanksgiving meal made the churches an unusual combination of formality and informality.

Hymns

There are many references to the singing of hymns in the churches of the Messiah (1 Cor. 14:26; Col. 3:16–17; Eph. 5:18–20; Jas 5:14; Acts 16:25). The Roman governor Pliny reported to the emperor Trajan that the Christians 'chanted hymns to Christ as if to a god' (*Epistles* 10.96.7).[3]

Scholars have identified passages in the texts of the New Testament that have been adapted from church hymns (e.g. Phil. 2:6–11; Col. 1:15–20; John 1:1–18; Eph. 5:14; 1 Tim. 3:16; many passages in the Apocalypse). The Psalms were probably a pattern and inspiration for these hymns. A striking characteristic of the hymns was their focus on Christ. The hymns were not general expressions of praise to God but specifically 'sung to' Christ in praise of him.

Welfare

These churches were earthly manifestations of their heavenly Lord. Since considered together they were his 'body', it was vital that they expressed practical care for one another, especially to those who were poor and in need: widows, orphans and the diseased and disabled. Church elders visited the sick in their homes, anointing them with oil and praying over them (Jas 5:14–15). Wealthier members were expected to contribute generously for needs, and 'deacons' and 'almoners' were appointed to distribute money and food (Rom. 12:7–8; 1 Pet. 4:10). Inevitably, there were abuses of this generosity; for example, by younger widows (1 Tim. 5:3–16).

Evangelism

Members of these churches were expected to seek the salvation of others, including as yet unconverted spouses (1 Cor. 7:16; 1 Pet. 3:1–2). Furthermore, all believers were expected to conduct themselves both consistently and sensitively to 'win' outsiders for faith in the Messiah Jesus (1 Cor. 10:31 – 11:1; Col. 4:5).

Additionally, however, some members engaged in public preaching; for example, in the marketplace (e.g. Phil. 4:2–3; 1 Thess. 1:6–7). Merchants, soldiers, public officials who were believers took the message of the Messiah with them on their travels (Acts 19:10). We note the travels of merchant tent-makers Priscilla and Aquila from Rome to Corinth to Ephesus back to Rome and then to Ephesus again.[4] Evangelists went out from churches and through their preaching established other churches (e.g. Col. 1:7; 4:12; 1 Pet. 1:12, 23). And so the message of the Messiah spread rapidly throughout the Roman world.

Summary

The years following the Messiah's historical lifespan witnessed the remarkable spread of the message and the formation of groups of believers who gathered regularly in the homes of wealthier members. While these churches had (male) elders, these leaders do not appear to have been bureaucratic or authoritarian. The social barriers of wealth, status, gender or slavery do not appear to have impeded their unity, found 'in Christ' and focused towards Christ, the Lord. The genuineness of their faith and love and the spontaneity of their worship of the Lord appear to have attracted many new members. Admission to the groups was by means of careful instruction followed by baptism. Fundamental to their life together were invocation to the Lord, prayer to 'Abba, Father', the singing of hymns to the Lord, the sharing in the thanksgiving meal and the care of needy members.

Conclusion

The rapid spread of the message of the Messiah and the formation of Messiah groups (churches) was a direct consequence of his
brief historical appearance. The impact of those few years was
demonstrated concretely in the rise of the Messiah movement. Yet
their experience of his heaven-sent Spirit was no less palpable as
they gathered to sing their praises to the risen and exalted Lord.
Spirit-inspired messianic enthusiasm was the engine that drove the
remarkable growth of earliest Christianity.

Yet this post-resurrection adoration of the Lord is inconceivable apart from the powerful conviction of the original disciples
that the pre-resurrection Jesus was a deity figure. The resurrection
was merely the confirmation of who he had been and what he had
done beforehand as the Son of the Father who had sent him.

17. HOSTILE WITNESSES

The three earliest non-Christian witnesses to Jesus the Christ and the early Christians were Josephus, Pliny and Tacitus. We are interested to know how these writers think about Christ and Christians. Are they sympathetic or hostile, and do they contradict or corroborate what we find in the writings of the earliest Christians?

Josephus

Born circa 37 of aristocratic parents in Jerusalem, Josephus became the military leader defending Galilee from the invading Romans in AD 66–67, but was captured by the future emperor, the general Vespasian. Throughout the remainder of the war he served Vespasian and his son Titus as interpreter and adviser. After the war, Vespasian adopted Josephus as a member of the Flavian dynasty so that he became known as Flavius Josephus. Vespasian, his sons the emperors Titus and Domitian, sustained Josephus in a villa in Rome and provided him with financial support to write his propagandist work the *Jewish War*.

In the nineties Josephus wrote his massive history of the Jewish people, *Jewish Antiquities*, where he mentions Jesus and his brother James:

> About this time there lived Jesus, a wise man [if indeed one ought to call him a man]. For he was one who wrought surprising feats and was a teacher of such people who accept the truth gladly. He won over many Jews and many of the Greeks. [He was the Christ.] When Pilate, upon hearing him accused by men of the highest standing amongst us had condemned him to be crucified, those who had in the first place come to love him did not give up their affection for him. [On the third day he appeared to them restored to life, for the prophets of God had prophesied these and countless other marvellous things about him.] And the tribe of Christians, so called after him, has still to this day not disappeared. (*Jewish Antiquities* 18.63–64)[1]

> Ananus [Annas] thought he had a favourable opportunity because Festus was dead and Albinus was still on his way. So he convened the judges of the Sanhedrin and brought before them a man named James, the brother of Jesus who was called Christ, and certain others. He accused them of having transgressed the law and delivered them up to be stoned. Those of the inhabitants of the city who were considered the most fair-minded and who were strict in observance of the law were offended at this. They therefore secretly sent to King Agrippa urging him, for Ananus had not even been correct in his first step . . . King Agrippa, because of Ananus' actions, deposed him from the high priesthood . . . (*Jewish Antiquities* 20.200–201, 203)[2]

The James passage states that Jesus was 'called Christ' or 'said to be Christ', which calls into question the Jesus passage that declares without qualification that Jesus 'was the Christ'. This suggests that the Jesus passage may have been interpolated with non-Josephan words about Jesus, as bracketed in the passage above. The third-century Christian writer Origen specifically states that Josephus did not regard Jesus as the Messiah. Yet the emended text appears exactly in the Christian historian Eusebius' writing in the first quarter of the fourth century. It seems that a Christian had beefed up Josephus' text some time between Origen and Eusebius.

The James passage appears to be free of interpolation. When we remove the interpolations from the first passage and consider it with the second passage we discover useful information about Jesus:

- Jesus was a rabbi ('wise man') of some kind, who worked miracles.
- He was *said to be* the Messiah (by his followers).
- He was executed by Pilate (AD 26–36) at request of leading Jews.
- Jesus had a brother named James (executed by the high priest in 62).
- 'The tribe of Christians' had still not died out when Josephus wrote in the nineties.

Josephus' words are a true reflection of the things he would have observed about early Christianity as a young man in Palestine who later lived in Rome, where the Christians survived Nero's assault on them in AD 64–65 (see below). Josephus is clearly no Christian, yet accurately portrays Christ, his execution and the survival of Christianity.

Tacitus

Cornelius Tacitus (c. 56–120) served as consul in Rome in 97 and proconsul of Roman Asia 112–113. His major work *The Annals of Imperial Rome* covers the eras of Emperors Tiberius, Gaius, Claudius and Nero in eighteen books, of which only books 1–4 (Tiberius) and 12–15 (Claudius and Nero) are intact.

The passage following is part of his lengthy account of the fire in AD 64 that raged for six days, leaving only four of the fourteen districts of Rome undestroyed (bk. 15, chs. 38–45). In the weeks after the fire, many came to believe Nero had ordered the torching of the city so as to rebuild it on a grand scale. To counteract these suspicions Nero engaged in ambitious building projects and elaborate religious sacrifices to appease the gods, but to no good effect. Because the rumours about him persisted, Nero arrested, tried and executed numerous Christians to deflect attention away from him:

But neither human help, nor imperial munificence, nor all the modes of placating Heaven could stifle or dispel the belief that the fire had taken place by order.

Therefore, to scotch the rumour, Nero substituted as culprits, and punished with the utmost refinements of cruelty, a class of men, loathed for their vices, whom the crowd styled Christians.

Christ, the founder of the name, had undergone the death penalty in the reign of Tiberius, by sentence of the procurator Pontius Pilate, and a pernicious superstition was checked for the moment, only to break out once more, not merely in Judea, the home of the disease, but in the capital itself, where all things horrible or shameful in the world collect and find a vogue.

First, then, the confessed members of the sect were arrested; next, on their disclosures, vast numbers were convicted, not so much on the count of arson as for hatred of the human race.

And derision accompanied their end; they were covered with wild beasts' skins and torn to death by dogs; or they were fastened on crosses, and when daylight failed were burned to serve as lamps by night.

Nero had offered his Gardens for the spectacle, and gave an exhibition in his Circus, mingling with the crowd in the habit of a charioteer, or mounted on his car. Hence, in spite of a guilt which had earned the most exemplary punishment, there arose a sentiment of pity, due to the impression that they were being sacrificed not for the welfare of the state but the ferocity of a single man. (Tacitus, *Annals of Imperial Rome* 15.44)[3]

As a former consul in Rome, Tacitus would have had access to official archives and may have seen Pilate's report to Tiberius about the execution of Jesus and others in Judea in AD 33. Tacitus' account, which appears not to have been corrupted, contains important information:

- Christians in Rome were scapegoats for Nero following the fire in AD 64 that destroyed ten of the fourteen districts of Rome.
- Tacitus says vast numbers of these Christians were convicted, not for arson but for 'hatred of the human race', a probable reference to their refusal to acknowledge the primacy of Rome and her emperor.

- Although these *Christians* were hated for the 'vices' (especially their nonconformity in Roman religious practices), the population felt sorry for them.
- Nero had large numbers crucified and daubed with tar and set alight.
- Tacitus digresses briefly to explain that (1) the *Christians* took their name from a certain *Christ* (a Jew?), (2) who was executed in Judea under Pontius Pilate, but (3) surprisingly *Christ's* movement (a Jewish sect?) 'broke out afresh' in Judea, and (4) his following spread from Judea to Rome. (Tacitus' version innocently confirms the resurrection-based 'breakout' narrated in the early chapter of the Acts of the Apostles.)

Tacitus is no Christian, yet his hostile information coincides with the New Testament's portrayal of Jesus as one whose followers proclaimed him to be the Christ, executed under Pilate but whose movement 'broke out afresh' and spread from Judea to Rome.

Pliny the Younger

Pliny the Younger (c. 61–112), formerly a consul in Rome, was sent circa 110 by the emperor Trajan to govern the disorganized province of Bithynia (south of the Black Sea). His correspondence with Trajan 110–112 is recorded in book 10 of his letters.

In letter 96 he reports on the rapid spread of Christianity in the province, both in rural and urbanized areas. Temples were abandoned and the businesses of those who sold fodder for sacrificial animals had been shut down though lack of demand.

Pliny interrogated those accused of being Christians and sentenced them to death if they insisted on saying they were, despite being asked the question three times. And he dispatched those who were Roman citizens to Rome for trial.

Others who were accused, however, acknowledged they had been Christians but no longer were. Pliny subjected them to a formal legal procedure. The accused were required to invoke the state gods according to Pliny's dictated statement, engage in an act of worship with incense to the emperor's image and also 'curse Christ'.

Pliny twice refers to Christ, but without further explanation. We reasonably assume that Pliny knew (but did not need to tell the emperor) that Christ had been executed in Judea some years before. Since his friend Tacitus (governor of neighbouring Asia) made this clear (as noted above), we assume it was common knowledge among Roman bureaucrats:

> They maintained that their guilt or error had amounted only to this: they had been in the habit of meeting on an appointed day before daybreak and singing a hymn antiphonally to Christ as if to a god, and binding themselves with an oath – not to commit any crime but to abstain from theft, robbery, and adultery, from breach of faith, and from repudiating a trust when called upon to honour it. After this ceremony, it had been their custom to disperse and reassemble to take food of a harmless kind . . . (Pliny, *Epistles* 10.96.7)[4]

Pliny provides us with useful information about early Christianity and Christian practices:

- Christians had become very numerous in Bithynia, since at least AD 90, so much so that many pagan temples had been closed.
- Their practices included meeting on a fixed day and chanting hymns to Christ 'as if *to* a god', confirming very early New Testament texts that Christians met to worship Christ, including by singing hymns *to* him as Lord.
- Christians viewed Christ above the emperor and the gods and would die rather than comply with Roman 'tests' of praying to statues of the emperor and the gods and cursing Christ.

Pliny the outside observer is deeply opposed to the Christians. Nonetheless, his portrayal of their dedication to Christ and their religious meetings is consistent with the Christians' own version of these things, as we find them in the New Testament.

Conclusion

These sources are particularly valuable because they were written by 'outsiders' hostile to the Christians. That is, they cannot be accused of pro-Christian bias. This is important, since our main sources in the Gospels and letters of the New Testament are all written by 'insiders' and are clearly Christian.

At no point of detail do these 'outside' sources contradict historical details in the New Testament. Rather, they confirm the 'raw facts' about the *who* (Christ), the *where* (Judea), the *when* (under Pilate) and the *what next* (the movement spread out from Judea into the Roman Empire, including Rome itself).

They confirm the New Testament's picture that the Roman authorities took a negative and punitive attitude to the followers of Christ.

Of great importance is Pliny's window into early Christian meetings, where people assembled weekly to worship this crucified man as if alive and a god. Pliny confirms the central claims of the New Testament that Jesus of Nazareth was crucified as the Messiah, but that he was resurrected and worshipped by his followers in assemblies called 'churches'.

It is striking that Josephus, Tacitus and Pliny each use *Christ* as a name, as the New Testament letters also frequently do. Yet it is evident from the Gospels that 'Christ' was initially a title, '*the* Christ' (Greek for '*the* Messiah'). The transition from a title to a name probably occurred because outsiders would have been bewildered by a title for someone as 'the smeared one' (the literal meaning of 'the Christ'). Nonetheless, the consistent non-Christian use of the words 'Christ' and 'Christian' preserve the original meaning of Jesus as the Messiah, whose followers were dubbed 'Messiah's men', 'Christians'. That the non-Christian witnesses never speak of 'Jesus' men' is also probably very significant. What mattered to people then was not so much Jesus' personal name (as the founder of the movement) but his implied title 'Christ' (Messiah) that identified his disciples as 'Christ's followers' (Greek, *Christianoi*).

18. CHRIST IN THE SECOND CENTURY

By the end of the second century as many as twelve known Gospels were in circulation.[1]

Throughout history, mainstream Christians have regarded the Gospels printed in our Bibles as the only valid sources of information about Jesus. Lately, however, some scholars have urged that other texts provide a more authentic portrayal of Jesus, in particular the *Gospel of Thomas*.

The question of genuine sources is critical, since we have no other way of knowing much about Jesus. The hostile witnesses Josephus, Tacitus and Pliny are useful in corroborating the broad picture from the Gospels but lack the details needed for an independent and coherent picture of Jesus and early Christianity.

But how do we distinguish between authentic and inauthentic gospels?

Authentic Gospels

Our methods of identifying authentic sources are based on straightforward historical procedures.

Witness of the earliest post-apostolic writers

We are fortunate in having texts from writers who immediately follow the New Testament era. These writers quote from, allude to or echo the majority of New Testament texts. See the table below.

Although the post-apostolic writers' references to New Testament texts tend to be rather free and brief, we can make two important observations.

The first is that the major texts of the New Testament, including the four Gospels, had been written and were in circulation and use by the end of the first century.[3] Accordingly, the earliness of *these* Gospels qualifies them to be regarded as primary sources for Jesus the Messiah. This has always been the view of mainstream

Clement (c. 95)	Didache (c. 90)	Ignatius (c. 110)
Matthew	Matthew	Matthew
Mark	Mark	Mark
Luke	Luke	Luke
		John[2]
Acts		
		Romans
1 Corinthians	1 Corinthians	1 Corinthians
Ephesians		
		Philippians
	1 Thessalonians	1 Thessalonians
	2 Thessalonians	
	1 Timothy	
Hebrews		
James		
1 Peter		
2 Peter		

Christians and of historians. The other so-called gospels are not referred to, either positively or negatively, in the early post-apostolic writings for a very simple reason: *they had not yet been written.*

Secondly, the post-apostolic writers' early endorsement of the letters of the New Testament indicates they believed the same as the apostles did about Jesus: he was the Messiah. The early acceptance of the *teachings* of the letters of the New Testament about Christ logically meant that the post-apostolic writers also accepted the Gospels' *narratives* about Jesus as the Messiah. This is confirmed in a mini-creed we find in Ignatius' writings:

> Jesus Christ . . . was of *the stock of David,*
> who was from Mary,
> who was truly born, ate and drank,
> was truly persecuted under Pontius Pilate,
> was truly crucified and died . . .
> who also was truly raised from the dead,
> His Father raising him . . .[4]

Ignatius' reference to 'the stock of David' is clear evidence of his commitment to Jesus as Messiah. Ignatius, a forthright leader, did not shrink from attacking any teaching that diminished Jesus. Had the extraneous gospels with their off-centre views of Jesus already been written, Ignatius would have identified and opposed them, so committed was he to Jesus as the Christ.

The above quotation from Ignatius shows that he followed the theological trajectory of the apostles before him. Similarly firm views are found in Polycarp, who wrote soon after Ignatius, and in Justin Martyr, who came after Polycarp.

In circa AD 110 Polycarp wrote:

> believing in him
> who raised our Lord Jesus Christ from the dead,
> and gave him glory and a throne at his right hand,
> > to whom are subjected all things in heaven and earth,
> > whom every breath of wind serves,
> > who will come as judge of living and dead.[5]

In circa 150 Justin wrote:

> Thus we are not atheists, since we worship
> the creator of this universe . . .
> and that with good reason honour
> him who taught us these things
> and was born for this purpose,
> Jesus Christ,
> who was crucified under Pontius Pilate,
> > the governor of Judea in the time of Tiberius Caesar,
> having heard that he is the Son of the true God
> and holding him in second rank,
> and the prophetic Spirit third in order,
> > we shall proceed to demonstrate.[6]

It is clear that the creedlike statements of Ignatius, Polycarp and Justin arose out of the earlier apostolic teaching about Jesus the Christ we find in the Gospels and letters. Furthermore, we can easily see that the Apostles' Creed and the Nicene Creed evolved from these early post-apostolic statements.

Specific early references to the Gospels

As we saw earlier, Papias, bishop of Hierapolis (Pamukkale in modern Turkey), writing in the first decades of the second century, quotes from one whom he calls the Elder, whose views went back well into the previous century. The Elder explains the origins of Mark's and Matthew's Gospels (reported in Eusebius, *History of the Church* 3.39.3–16). Furthermore, by asserting that Mark wrote 'accurately', Papias made an implicit reference to Luke (see Luke 1:1–4). As well, by giving the name of six disciples in the order they appear in the Gospel of John, Papias knows that Gospel also.[7] We can conclude that Papias referred directly to the origins of the Gospels of Mark and Matthew and indirectly to the Gospels of Luke and John. Papias' information confirms the point made above from the post-apostolic writings, that the four Gospels were in circulation by the end of the first century at the latest.

Gospel manuscripts

We are very fortunate that many portions of early Gospel manuscripts have survived the ravages of time.[8] The papyrus ($\mathcal{P}$)
fragments in the table below have been found in Egypt (where
there is minimal humidity). We know they were originally written
in codex (early book) form, since there is writing on the front and
back of the leaves.

Fragile papyri that have survived in the sands of Egypt are
evidence that John, Matthew and Luke were in circulation in the
early part of the second century and that all four canonical
Gospels were in circulation by the end of the second century.
These fragments were originally part of codices read in church
meetings from the end of the apostolic age. Conspicuously absent
is any surviving fragment of the Gospel of Mark. Yet Matthew's
and Luke's reproduction of Mark in the body of their Gospels, as
agreed by most scholars, establishes the prior existence of Mark.
While most surviving fragments of John come from the late
second century, the discovery of $\mathcal{P}^{52}$, dating from the beginning of
the second century, establishes a first-century origin for this
Gospel. Furthermore, the extensive parts of John in $\mathcal{P}^{90}$, $\mathcal{P}^{75}$, $\mathcal{P}^{66}$
and $\mathcal{P}^{45}$ support the widespread early use of this Gospel.

Papyrus	Date	Content
$\mathcal{P}^{52}$	Early 2nd C.	A few verses of John 18
$\mathcal{P}^{67}$	c. 125–150	A few verses from Matthew 3, 5
$\mathcal{P}^{64}$	c. 125–150	A few verses from Matthew 26
$\mathcal{P}^{4}$	c. 125–150	Portions of Luke 1, 2, 3, 4
$\mathcal{P}^{75}$	c. 175	Portions of Luke 3, 4, 5, 6, 7, 9, 17, 22 Much of John
$\mathcal{P}^{77}$	c. 175–200	A few verses of Matthew 23
$\mathcal{P}^{103}$	c. 175–200	A few verses from Matthew 13, 14
$\mathcal{P}^{104}$	c. 175–200	A few verses from Matthew 21
$\mathcal{P}^{90}$	c. 175–200	A portion of John 18 – 19
$\mathcal{P}^{1}$	c. 200	Portions of Matthew 1
$\mathcal{P}^{66}$	c. 200	Most of John
$\mathcal{P}^{45}$	Early 3rd C.	Portions of all four Gospels and Acts

Reading and quoting the Gospels

The earliest post-New Testament reference to the written Gospel is found in the *Didache* at the end of the first century. The next extant reference to 'gospel' is by Justin Martyr (c. 150), who refers to 'the memoirs composed by the [apostles], which are called *gospels* . . .' (Justin, *First Apology* 66–67).[9] Justin describes how the church leaders read and applied the message of the Gospels to the assembled believers each Sunday in every city.

Furthermore, in his extensive writings, Justin frequently echoes texts from each of the four Gospels.[10] We reasonably assume, therefore, that by his reference to 'gospels' Justin has in mind *these* Gospels.

Summary

The view of mainstream Christians as supported by scholarly research is that the four Gospels in our Bibles are the closest historically to Jesus, represent the views of his earliest followers and are, for these reasons, authentic. This conviction is based on the accumulated consideration of early referencing in the post-apostolic writing, specific identification of Gospels by name by the Elder (quoted by Papias) and by the plethora of early Gospel manuscript fragments.

Marcion

According to second-century mainstream leaders, the one who posed the greatest threat to the true church was Marcion of Sinope (a Black Sea port). Although often called a Gnostic, it appears that Marcion should be regarded more as a radical Paulinist who on that account rejected the Jewish law. Accordingly, he rejected the Jewish God as a mere *demiurge* (a secondary god) and not the one true, living God. Marcion came to Rome circa 144, though there is debate whether his idiosyncratic views were formulated there or beforehand. In his major work *Antitheses* Marcion rejected the God of the Old Testament and limited his recognition of New Testament writings to those that de-emphasized Christianity's Jewish roots as much as possible. Accordingly, Marcion accepted only an expurgated version of Luke's Gospel and limited versions of Paul's letters.

Excommunicated from the church in Rome, Marcion established a church of his own, which spread throughout the empire. In effect, Marcion created his own 'canon' of acceptable texts (Luke and Paul) as vehicles for his theological beliefs. Marcion's theological views and considerable ability in establishing a powerful rival church (based on ascetical principles) imposed great pressure on those who cast him out. His wholesale rejection of the Old Testament forced others to evaluate its place in the church's life and the relationship with Jesus' 'Father' as the Creator of the universe. Marcion's definition of texts acceptable to him forced the issue of 'canonicity' on the leaders in the next generation.

Other gospels

There are two classes of reference. First, the church fathers allude to gospels for which we have little or no direct evidence; that is, the *Gospel of the Ebionites*, the *Gospel of the Nazoreans* and the *Gospel of the Hebrews*. In the absence of passages from these texts, we can do little more than speculate as to their origin, character or content. These works appear to have been compiled for Jewish Christians known as Ebionites and Nazoreans, who probably continued Jewish practices (circumcision, sabbath and the calendar). The church fathers hint that these gospels are adaptations of Matthew (the most 'Jewish' of the Gospels).

The second category of reference consists of surviving papyri texts, such as Valentinus' *Gospel of Truth*, the 'Unknown Gospel', *The Gospel of Peter* and the *Gospel of Thomas*.

We can quickly eliminate Valentinus' *Gospel of Truth* from consideration. It has no narrative but is a meditation in which he freely adapts passages from the New Testament books, in particular John's Gospel and letters and Paul's letters. It can in no sense be called a 'gospel'.

The 'Unknown Gospel' is an important text, since it is confidently dated to the middle of the second century.[11] It consists of several short fragments of broken text cast in narrative form, so that it can be called a 'gospel'. It has connections with the canonical Gospels (including John's), is free of any explicitly heretical doctrine and lacks the exaggerations found in many second-century works (e.g. *Gospel of Peter*). The major issue, of course, is whether it is a source or a redaction of the canonical Gospels. The careful observation of E. C. Colwell should be noted: 'the new evangelist had read the fourfold gospel more than once and uses it as a source for his own work'.[12] The fragmentary remains of this 'Unknown Gospel' most probably suggest an early attempt at creating a Gospel harmony, anticipating the efforts of Justin Martyr, who created expanses of harmonized texts drawn from the canonical Gospels. These, in turn, anticipated Justin's pupil Tatian's full-scale harmony, the *Diatessaron* (see below).[13]

The Gospel of Peter is a second-century work identifiably in narrative format, chiefly related to the passion and resurrection of Christ. Although some have argued that the *Gospel of Peter* was a source of the Synoptic Gospels,[14] it is more probable that it is the opposite: an *adaptation* of the canonical Gospels.[15] Reasons to date it in the second century include its Docetic and Gnostic elements, its blurring of the lines between the 'Lord's' death and his ascension, the gargantuan height of the resurrected Jesus and the hagiographic character of the miracles. Peter Head concludes that 'the cumulative evidence for a second century date is strong and adds to the impression that the *Gospel of Peter* is a redaction of the canonical material'.[16]

The *Gospel of Thomas* does not belong to the gospel genre, since it is not a narrative but rather a series of sayings of Jesus. It is a fourth-century Coptic text that appears to have been translated from a second-century Greek version. The *Gospel of Thomas* is not a straight translation, however, since in the intervening century the Coptic version seems to have assimilated to the Coptic version of the New Testament. Consequently, we cannot confidently retrovert the Coptic version back to a second-century Greek original. In effect, we are left with the fourth-century version.

Many sayings bear close similarity to sayings of Jesus in the Synoptic Gospels. So the burning question is, 'Did the *Gospel of*

Thomas depend on the canonical Gospels or was it written independently of them?' The issue is complex and scholars are divided, though most hold Thomas to be a redaction of Matthew, Luke and John.

The main argument for the independence of the *Gospel of Thomas* is that its order differs from the Gospels. If it is dependent, so the argument runs, why does it change the Synoptics' order? Against this, however, it is pointed out that the order of the earlier Greek fragments is different from the Coptic version, so that *Thomas'* original sequence is unknown. Furthermore, the sequence of the Coptic *Gospel of Thomas* appears to follow an idiosyncratic structure as dictated by link words. It has to be asked which is the more probable: that Matthew, Luke and John have each somehow rearranged and reordered the *Gospel of Thomas* to create their own Gospels, or that the author of the *Gospel of Thomas* has thematically selected and given Gnostic colouring to passages from the canonical Gospels? The latter option is clearly preferable.

See the parallels between the Gospels of Matthew, Luke and John and the *Gospel of Thomas* in the table below.

Where cases like *Thomas'* parable of the sower are studied, it points to 'a 'gnosticising redaction of the synoptic parable'.[17] The

Matthew	Thomas	Luke	Thomas	John	Thomas
5:10	69a	11:27–28	79	1:9	24
5:14	32	12:13–14	72	1:14	28
6:2–4	6, 14	12:16–21	63	4:13–15	13
6:3	62	12:49	10	7:32–36	38
7:6	93	17:20–21	3	8:12; 9:5	77
10:16	39				
11:30	90				
13:24–30	57				
13:44	109				
13:45–46	76				
13:47–50	8				
15:13	40				
18:20	30				
23:13	39, 102				

critical thing is that this kind of Gnostic thought emerged only in the second century.

While some have hoped that the *Gospel of Thomas* would prove to predate the Gospels and reveal new information about Jesus, the evidence points rather to the significance of this text as a window into second-century Gnostic Christianity. In any case, it is a fourth-century Coptic text whose connections with its second-century Greek antecedent remain problematic.

Dates of second-century gospels (approximate)

120	150	160	180
Gospel of Nazoreans	*Papyrus Egerton 2*	*Gospel*	*Gospel of*
Gospel of the Ebionites	*Gospel of Truth(?)*	*of Peter*	*Thomas*

My conclusion is that the *Gospel of the Nazoreans* and the *Gospel of the Ebionites*, the *Gospel of Truth*, the *Gospel of Peter*, the 'Unknown Gospel' and the *Gospel of Thomas* all prove to be of second-century origin. In each case their similarities to the canonical Gospels are best explained by their dependency on them. The *Gospel of the Nazoreans*, the *Gospel of the Ebionites* and the 'Unknown Gospel' generally reproduce Matthew with a markedly Jewish interest. On the other hand, the *Gospel of Peter* appears to be a Gnosticized version of Mark, and the *Gospel of Truth* and *Gospel of Thomas* are not cast as narratives and should not be called 'gospels'.[18] We are able to eliminate each of these as primary sources of information for the works of the historical Christ, although possibly some genuine words of Jesus have survived in the *Gospel of Thomas*, though distorted by Gnostic ideas.

The fourfold Gospel (c. 150–180)

The crisis created by Marcion's emasculated gospel and the Gnostics' multiplication of gospels in the first part of the second century forced the church leaders in the years following to make the authentic fourfold Gospel explicit. Previously, it had probably been more or less assumed, though possibly with a degree of toleration of other texts. The rival churches established by gifted leaders like Marcion and Valentinus forced the issue of canonical definition.

Irenaeus: the fourfold Gospel

Irenaeus, a native of Roman Asia who later became a missionary in southern Gaul, understood well that he was joined to the apostolic age through his mentor, Polycarp, bishop of Smyrna:

> Polycarp . . . was not only instructed by apostles, and conversed with many who had seen Christ, but was also by apostles in Asia appointed bishop in the church in Smyrna, whom I also saw in my early youth.
>
> [Polycarp] . . . always taught the things he had learned from the apostles, and which the church has handed down and which alone are true. To these things all the Asiatic churches testify, as do those who have succeeded Polycarp . . . a man who was of greater weight, and a man of more steadfast witness of truth than Valentinus and Marcion and the rest of the heretics. (Irenaeus, *Against Heresies* 3.3.4)[19]

It is important to connect Irenaeus' conviction about the 'true' apostolic Gospels with his sense of unbroken continuity with the era of the apostles, through the human link Polycarp.[20] Furthermore, we must notice that Irenaeus measured the novelties of Valentinus and Marcion against Polycarp, who had been 'instructed by apostles'.[21]

Irenaeus' two chief enemies, then, were Marcion and Valentinus, whose theological errors were expressed in their views about authoritative texts. Marcion articulated his version of Christianity by *reducing* the extant Gospels to one, a severely edited Luke. For his part Valentinus stated his revised Christianity in '*more* gospels than there really are', including by writing a gospel of his own that was a radical reinterpretation of the apostolic texts.

In his work *Against Heresies* (written c. 180) Irenaeus famously insists against the various Gnostic gospels that there can be only four authentic Gospels: 'it is not possible that the gospels can be either *more* or *fewer* in number than they are' (*Against Heresies* 3.11.6).[22] At the same time he speaks of the one Gospel as *quadriform* (*euangelion tetramorphon*): 'For the living creatures [of

Revelation] are *quadriform*, and the gospel is *quadriform* . . .' (*Against Heresies* 3.11.8).[23]

Probably, Irenaeus' contention that the *one* true Gospel is *quadriform* was not a novelty, but a reassertion of an established view that went back to Justin Martyr or earlier. Consistent with this, and more probable than not, Irenaeus and those before him had already begun to use one codex for church reading in place of four (bulky) individual Gospel scrolls.[24] The location of four Gospels in one codex along with the assertion that the one Gospel was found only in four Gospels was a potent assertion of the authenticity and authority of these texts as apostolic.

A mark of Irenaeus' conviction of the 'canonical' *fourfold* Gospel is his account of their origin:

> *Matthew* composed his gospel among the Hebrews in their language, when Peter and Paul were preaching the gospel in Rome and founding the church [there]. After their death, *Mark*, the disciple of Peter, handed down to us the preaching of Peter in written form. *Luke*, the companion of Paul, set down the gospel preached by him in a book. Finally, *John* the disciple of the Lord, who also reclined on his breast, himself composed the gospel when he was living in Ephesus [in the province of Asia].
> (*Against Heresies* 3.1.1)[25]

We may quibble over Irenaeus' account of the origins of the Gospels, but his conviction of their delimited *fourfold* character is reinforced by his explanation of their beginnings.

Superscriptions

Irenaeus' assertion of the *one* Gospel in *four* Gospels was also anticipated in the superscriptions of the Gospels. Their superscriptions are always the same: *Gospel according to Matthew*, *Gospel according to Mark*, *Gospel according to Luke* and *Gospel according to John*. This pattern of uniformity was not due to church synods, which did not appear until later in the second century. It is reasonable to argue that the format of the superscriptions (*Gospel according to* . . .) and the use of the one codex for four Gospels arose in Rome early in the second century, and were disseminated from there,

influenced by the eminence of the world capital and the importance of its church.

This 'one Gospel through four Gospels' is confirmed by the
Muratorian Canon, originating a decade or so after Irenaeus' *Against
Heresies*. The opening line of the intact text begins, 'The third book
of the gospel, according to Luke', implying two prior 'books'.
Following the comments about Luke, the *Canon* continues, 'The
fourth gospel is by John, one of the disciples.' The point to notice
is that the gospel is a *single* entity of which there are four 'books' or
'gospels', each written 'according to . . .' a named evangelist. This
formula is confirmed by the earlier papyri manuscripts and by references in the church fathers.

Tatian: one Gospel 'through four'

For Irenaeus, the *one Gospel that was also four* (neither more nor less)
was his response to the claims of Marcion's gospel and the
Gnostics' gospels. For Tatian, however, the principle of multiple
Gospels was not a solution but a problem. Even in those pre-
critical times many were perplexed over the verbal contradictions
between these texts.

Tatian, a disciple of Justin Martyr in Rome, later returned to his
native Assyria after his master's martyrdom in AD 165. Tatian's
solution to the discrepancies between the Gospels was to 'unpick'
and then 'restitch' them together in chronological order as one
entity, which became known as *The Diatessaron* (meaning 'through
four'). Tatian used the Gospel of John as the broad framework for
his harmonized gospel, into which he inserted Matthew, Mark and
Luke. Tatian *composed* in some way a combination and collection of
the Gospels, and *gave* this the name of *The Diatessaron* (Eusebius,
History of the Church 4.29.6).[26] Tatian's *Diatessaron* corroborates the
essential and exclusive fourfold nature of the one Gospel of
Christ.

Papyrus 45

Dramatic archaeological evidence for the fourfold Gospel was discovered in 1931 in a Coptic graveyard in Middle Egypt, where

eight manuscripts stored in jars were found. Five were manuscripts of various books of the Old Testament. Three, however, were texts of the New Testament, each a codex (early book) rather than a scroll. The first was a codex of the four Gospels and the Acts (known as Papyrus 45), the second, a codex of Paul's letters (known as Papyrus 46) and the third, a codex of Revelation (Papyrus 47).

$\mathcal{P}^{45}$ as a collection of texts in a codex or 'book' indicates that they had been used in church gatherings for public reading. The codex was also easier to store than the scroll as well as cheaper, since the leaves (pages) could be written on both sides. The overwhelming majority of surviving early papyri of texts of the New Testament were written in codex format.

The significance of $\mathcal{P}^{45}$ is that it is the earliest collection of all four Gospels and is dated to the first part of the third century.

Summary: the fourfold Gospel

Irenaeus and Tatian faced different problems that were, respectively, the *number* of authentic Gospels and *discrepancies* between the four true Gospels. Outwardly, their responses were different. Yet Irenaeus' *quadriform* Gospel and Tatian's *Diatessaron* both sought to defend the common conviction that Matthew, Mark, Luke and John were the only authentic apostolic Gospels.

Conclusion

I conclude that the four Gospels in our Bibles belong to the first century and are the only 'gospels' that qualify for this early dating. The implications of this are considerable: chiefly, that the four Gospels were in use in the churches within *six decades* of Jesus.

From the early decades of the second century, however, there were various attempts to change the message of those Gospels, whether by radically reducing their content (Marcion) or by adding extra texts (e.g. *Gospel of Thomas*). The insistence on the fourfold Gospel by Irenaeus, Tatian, the *Muratorian Canon*, and the Codex $\mathcal{P}^{45}$ represents the continuing conviction by later second-century mainstream leaders about the unique authority of Matthew, Mark, Luke and John.

By their commitment to the four Gospels the leaders of the churches in the second century maintained the messianic faith of Jesus himself and his immediate followers.

19. REFLECTION

Our words 'Christian' and 'Christianity' derive from the person named Christ, Greek for the original Hebrew word 'Messiah'. At the beginning, however, Jesus was known by his title *the* Christ (*the* Messiah). For convenience this title soon became Jesus' surname. Throughout this book I have often preferred to refer to the more original term Jesus *the Messiah*.

As Messiah, Jesus is the centre of the Bible's story, which is the story of God's salvation of the human race. As the fulfilment of the messianic promises in the Old Testament, the Messiah is the end of the beginning. At the same time, as the herald and inaugurator of the kingdom of God he is the beginning of the end. So Messiah is the centre of all things that matter, the end of the beginning and the beginning of the end both for humanity and for individuals.

Because he is central in God's good purposes, he claims the attention and loyalty of all people everywhere. Prophetically, Psalm 2 calls on each of us to *embrace* the Messiah because he is the Lord's king, his anointed One, concluding, 'Blessed are all who take refuge in him' (v. 11).

Some who reject that challenge think the witness of the New Testament is seriously flawed, suggesting that the pre-crucifixion Jesus was merely a gifted teacher or prophet and that the belief he was the Messiah was mistaken, whether innocently or wilfully.

Let me mention three historically secure facts and then raise an important issue.

First, it is a fact that the four recognized Gospels were written within sixty years of Jesus and that the *Gospel of Thomas* and other 'gospels' were rewritten versions of the authentic Gospels, produced later to propagate deviant versions of Christianity. This has always been and remains the consensus view of reputable scholars. Current fascination with the *Gospel of Thomas* is explained by the desire of some for a more Gnostic, mystical Jesus in line with the present spirit of the age.

The large number of surviving manuscripts of the Gospels in several languages and found in many places around the Mediterranean makes it possible for textual scholars to establish Gospel texts almost identical to what was originally written. The extensive quotation of portions of the Gospels in the church fathers (called 'citations') strengthens the ability of the scholars to determine textual accuracy.

Secondly, the hostile witnesses Josephus, Tacitus and Pliny in no way undermine, but in fact reinforce, the impression the New Testament gives us about Christ in Judea, his execution under Pilate, the dissemination of Christians throughout the empire and their worship of Christ, which was matched by their refusal to worship the gods or the emperor. Despite negative references to this movement as a spreading disease, the raw facts from these extra-biblical witnesses strikingly confirm the New Testament's accounts.

Thirdly, it is beyond dispute that the early Christians invoked the post-resurrection Christ as 'Lord', singing hymns to him and calling on him to 'come back' to them. Pliny's report to the emperor confirms the Christians met on a fixed day weekly when they sang hymns to Christ, as if to a god.

These are the facts. Now for the issue or challenge these facts imply: What manner of man was Jesus before his crucifixion so that immediately afterwards his disciples worshipped him? Most who think about this issue but who reject his claims tend to regard him as a lesser figure, a gifted teacher or prophet, but at the same time a good person. But the awkward thing is that his disciples, all Jews and forbidden to worship anyone but the Lord God, began to worship Jesus as Lord *immediately*. The difficulty is to explain *why* they did this.

This is the problem I have raised throughout the book. You will recall my approach, which attempts to be historically based. Noting as many as five discrete primary sources (Mark, John, Q, L, M), I have pointed out how these independently attest Jesus' sense of identity as Messiah, his mission, his teaching, his miracles and his consciousness of deity. My line of argument is that the historical Jesus, the Jesus before his crucifixion, was himself convinced he was the prophesied Messiah and that his disciples also came to be convinced he was the Messiah.

The Jewish leadership found him guilty of claiming to be the Messiah and the Romans crucified him as self-proclaimed king of the Jews, which was their understanding of a man's claim to be the Messiah.

The resurrection of Jesus, though the defining fact on which Christianity stands or falls, did not of itself introduce the idea that Jesus was the Messiah. Rather, his resurrection confirmed what Jesus and the Twelve already held to be true.

The issue for us is the same as it was to those identifiably ordinary men who accompanied Jesus around the hills surrounding the Sea of Tiberias. He did not tell them in as many words who he was, but rather asked them who *they* thought he was, based on what they had seen him do and heard him say.

Through the pages of the Gospels he asks us the same question, 'Who do *we* say he is?', and awaits our reply. But we should think carefully before we say he is merely a prophet or a good man. From investigating the facts of history, as outlined in this book, my own conviction is that 'Messiah' is the only intelligent response to give him, and that to embrace him, as Psalm 2 advises, is the wisest thing a human being can do.

NOTES

Chapter 1

1. Unless stated otherwise, all italics in quoted text are mine.
2. This section owes much to an unpublished paper by Dr J. Dickson, 'The Nouveaux Atheists', delivered at Macquarie University, Sydney (10 May 2008).
3. C. Hitchens, *God Is Not Great: How Religion Poisons Everything* (New York: Twelve, 2007), p. 122.
4. R. Dawkins, *The God Delusion* (London: Bantam, 2006), p. 96.
5. Ibid., p. 94.
6. Ibid., p. 250.
7. Ibid., p. 257.
8. Ibid., p. 97.
9. See generally, R. A. Burridge, *What Are the Gospels: A Comparison with Graeco-Roman Biography* (Cambridge: Cambridge University Press, 1992).
10. M. Onfray, *Atheist Manifesto* (New York: Arcade, 2005), p. xi.
11. Quoted in P. Copan (ed.), *Will the Real Jesus Please Stand Up* (Grand Rapids: Baker Books, 1998), p. 24.
12. E.g. in Matt. 16:21–25, the author depends on Mark 8:31 – 9:1, but also includes his own information: that Peter pleaded with Jesus, 'God forbid, Lord! This shall never happen to you' (Matt. 16:22). It appears that while Mark was depending on an eyewitness (Peter), Matthew *was himself* an eyewitness who recalled Peter's heartfelt plea.
13. I am assuming that John, writer of the Gospel and the letters, also wrote the Revelation, though this is not a universally held view.

Chapter 2

1. The well-known verdict of the noted Shakespearian commentator George Steevens (1736–1800). See W. Bryson, *Shakespeare* (London: HarperPress, 2007), p. 7.

Chapter 3

1. These are found in the Palestinian versions of the *Nineteen Benedictions*, quoted in G. Vermes, *Jesus the Jew* (Glasgow: Collins, 1973), p. 130.
2. See e.g. Ps. 45:6–7, probably addressed to David, whose throne endures for ever.
3. (I have sometimes laid out quotations differently from the style in the RSV.) For discussion of references in the Old Testament to the word *'almâ* (virgin), in particular in Gen. 24:43, Exod. 2:8 and Song 6:8, see J. A. Motyer, *The Prophecy of Isaiah* (Leicester: IVP, 1993), pp. 84–85.
4. How are we to explain the *two* messiahs of Qumran, in which the Priest-Messiah appears to have priority? The answer is that a Davidic Messiah was 'a relatively stable core' belief within Judaism between the testaments, but that the very rationale of a separatist group like the Qumran Essenes meant giving priority to a Messiah who was a *priest*. The Essenes had separated from Hasmonean society because the Hasmonean priesthood was corrupt and in need of purification.
5. J. H. Charlesworth, *The Old Testament Pseudepigrapha* (London: Darton Longman & Todd, 1983), p. 550. 'The lion of the tribe of Judah, the root of David' in Rev. 5:5 draws upon the same imagery as *4 Ezra*.
6. Ibid., p. 667.
7. J. Bowker, *The Targums and the Rabbinic Literature* (Cambridge: Cambridge University Press, 1969), p. 284.

Chapter 4

1. Tr. B. Radice, Loeb Classical Library (Cambridge, Mass.: William Heinemann, 1969), p. 289.
2. M. Smith, *Jesus the Magician* (New York: Harper & Row, 1978).

3. G. Vermes, *Jesus the Jew* (Glasgow: Collins, 1973).

4. The Cynic philosophy was founded centuries earlier in Greece by Diogenes of Sinope, who taught his followers to preach against the materialism of the majority. Their critics disparagingly called them 'cynics', based on the Greek word *kyōn* (dog). It is possible that the spread of Greek thought following Alexander's conquests brought the Cynics' teaching to Palestine.

5. J. D. Crossan, *The Historical Jesus: The Life of a Mediterranean Jewish Peasant* (San Francisco: HarperSanFrancisco, 1991).

6. J. D. Crossan, *The Birth of Christianity: Discovering What Happened in the Years Immediately After the Execution of Jesus* (San Francisco: HarperCollins, 1998), p. ix.

7. See P. Barnett, *The Birth of Christianity* (Grand Rapids: Eerdmans, 2005), pp. 55–78.

8. Quoted in M. Hengel, *Studies in Early Christology* (Edinburgh: T. & T. Clark, 1995), p. 19.

Chapter 5

1. Jesus is echoing Jer. 7:11 and Isa. 56:7.

2. Josephus, who wrote from Rome in the last thirty years of the first century, narrates the preaching of Jesus ben Ananias, who spoke against the temple but was released following scourging (*Jewish War* 6.300–309).

3. *Christianos* is a Latinism, whose suffix *-ianos* is a Greek form of the Latin *-ianus* and indicates a follower of a named leader.

4. D. G. Horrell, 'The Label *Christianos*: 1 Peter 4:16 and the Formation of Christian Identity', *Journal of Biblical Literature* 126 (2007), pp. 362–367.

5. Tr. K. Lake, Loeb Classical Library (Cambridge, Mass.: William Heinemann, 1992), pp. 297–298.

6. The home of Mark's mother, Mary, was the meeting place of early Christians in Jerusalem, where Peter was the leader (Acts 12:12). Mark, cousin of Barnabas, accompanied Paul and Barnabas on mission work in Cyprus and Anatolia (Acts 13:5). Later, he returned to Cyprus with Barnabas (Acts 15:39) before reappearing in Roman Asia (Col. 4:10). And then Mark was in Rome with Peter (1 Pet. 5:13). Our last glimpse of Mark is in Ephesus with Timothy (2 Tim. 4:11).

7. See further M. Hengel, *The Four Gospels and the One Gospel of Jesus Christ* (ET London: SCM, 2000), pp. 82–86; R. Bauckham, *Jesus and the Eyewitnesses* (Grand Rapids: Eerdmans, 2006), pp. 124–127.

8. Bauckham, *Eyewitnesses*, pp. 132–145, explores evidence from the ancient writers Lucian and Porphyry, where the key character appears at the beginning and end as the focus of the readers' attention, especially as an eyewitness source.

9. Ibid., p. 146.

10. H. W. Hoehner, *Herod Antipas: A Contemporary of Jesus Christ* (Grand Rapids: Zondervan, 1980), p. 317.

11. The list of withdrawals includes Mark 1:45; 3:7; 6:31–32; 6:45, 53; 7:24; 7:31; 8:10; 8:22; 9:30, 33.

12. Some ancient manuscripts have 'moved with wrath', which is not so well attested.

Chapter 6

1. The divergences presented an apologetic problem as early as the second century, when Julius Africanus (AD 160–240) felt compelled to provide an explanation of the differences between the lists in Matthew and Luke (quoted in Eusebius *History of the Church* 1.7–8). Julius Africanus notes that Herod had registers of Jewish families destroyed – to hide his lack of Jewish descent ('Herod . . . had no drop of Israelitish blood'). However, the relatives of Jesus in Nazareth were among those who managed to preserve the private records of their genealogies, which in their case showed Jesus' descent from David. According to Africanus, these records explained that the differences between the genealogies of Matthew and Luke were due to numbers of childless widows who married brothers of former husbands in accordance with the so-called levirate marriage provision (where a man died without a son to carry forward his name, the brother of the deceased was to sire a son to the widow). Thus some children were registered in the name of the 'legal' father, while others were registered in the name of an uncle who was not the biological father. 'Thus neither gospel is in error . . . Thus both accounts are perfectly true, bringing the line down to Joseph in a manner complex perhaps but certainly accurate'

(tr. K. Lake, Loeb Classical Library [Cambridge, Mass.: William Heinemann, 1992], p. 57). Africanus gives a detailed harmonization of the two lists, based on the preserved traditions of the Nazareth relatives of Jesus.

2. J. Finegan, *The Archeology of the New Testament* (Princeton: Princeton University Press, 1969), p. 29.

3. See B. Pixner, *With Jesus through Galilee* (Rosh Pina: Corazim, 1992), p. 17, referring to the archaeological work of B. Bagatti.

4. The Hebrew consonants of *nṣr*, 'branch', correspond phonetically with the Greek *nzr* in the word *Nazōraiōs*. The believers in Jerusalem led by James, the brother of Jesus, were later derisively spoken of as 'the sect of the *Nazōraiōn*' (Acts 24:5).

5. Contra J. J. Rousseau and R. Arav, *Jesus and His World* (Minneapolis: Fortress, 1995), p. 214, who think Nazareth may have taken its name from the Hebrew root *nāṣar*, 'watch' or 'guard' (Nazareth is in an elevated location).

6. According to *The Protevangelium of James*, Mary's parents were Joachim and Anna.

7. It is possible to read Matthew's account to suggest that Joseph and Mary lived in Judea prior to the birth of Jesus, and that they settled in Nazareth only after their return from Egypt (Matt. 2:1, 13, 22–23).

8. Tr. K. Lake, Loeb Classical Library (Cambridge, Mass.: William Heinemann, 1992), p. 253.

9. See further, D. S. Huffman, 'Genealogy', in J. B. Green and S. McKnight (eds.), *Dictionary of Jesus and the Gospels* (Downers Grove: IVP; Leicester: IVP, 1992), pp. 253–258. From Jesus' own day there was a polemical tradition that implied he was the fruit of an illegitimate union. His opponents said, '*We* were not born of fornication,' implying that Jesus *was* (John 8:41). The anti-Christian Celsus and various later Jewish sources claim that Mary became pregnant by a Roman soldier, Pandera (or Panthera). In 1859 a tombstone was found in Bingersbrück, Germany, of a Roman archer, Pantera, who had been posted at Sidon at some stage in his military career. See further, J. J. Rousseau and R. Arav, *Jesus and His World* (Minneapolis: Fortress, 1995), pp. 223–225.

10. Both Luke and Paul probably echo Isa. 7:14; 9:6.

Chapter 7

1. Quoted in A. M. Hunter, *Interpreting the Parables* (London: SCM, 1960), pp. 114–115.
2. Mark uses the word *kairos*, meaning a 'special moment', rather than *chronos*, meaning 'ordinary time'.
3. It is, nonetheless, an illuminating sideshow that establishes important milestones in salvation history; e.g. that John the Baptist began preaching in c. 28 and that Paul arrived in Corinth in c. 50. Reciprocally, salvation history can inform world history at certain points; e.g. that Caiaphas was son-in-law of the patriarchal high priest, Annas. It is important for scholars of salvation history to be well informed about the world history through which biblical history passed.
4. Quoted in Hunter, *Parables*, p. 113.
5. Quoted in H. K. McArthur and R. M. Johnson, *They Also Taught in Parables: Rabbinic Parables from the First centuries of the Christian Era* (Grand Rapids: Eerdmans, 1990), p. 63. Although dated to AD 200, it probably rests on earlier parables with a similar theme.
6. Although dated to AD 150, it probably rests on earlier traditions.
7. Quoted in McArthur and Johnson, *They Also Taught in Parables*, p. 68.

Chapter 8

1. H. Danby, *The Mishnah* (Oxford: Clarendon, 1933), p. 198.
2. For a list of miracles, see R. H. Fuller, *Interpreting the Miracles* (London: SCM, 1963), pp. 126–127.
3. Tr. L. Feldmann, Loeb Classical Library (Cambridge, Mass.: William Heinemann, 1965), p. 49.
4. I. Epstein, *The Babylonian Talmud Translated into English* (London: Soncino, 1935–52). For further (late) Jewish references to Jesus' miracles, see B. Blackburn, 'The Miracles of Jesus', in C. A. Evans and B. Chilton (eds.), *Studying the Historical Jesus* (Leiden: Brill, 1994), p. 361.
5. J. Jeremias, *New Testament Theology*, vol. 1 (ET London: SCM, 1971), p. 21.
6. The text as printed has been reconstructed.
7. B. Blackburn, 'The Miracles of Jesus', in Evans and Chilton, *Studying the Historical Jesus*, p. 356.

8. J. P. Meier, *A Marginal Jew: Rethinking the Historical Jesus*, vol. 2 (New York: Doubleday, 1994), p. 631.

9. For a review of those who doubt the truth of the miracles, see Blackburn, 'Miracles', pp. 363–368.

10. N. Perrin, *Rediscovering the Teaching of Jesus* (New York: Harper & Row, 1967), p. 136; also B. Mack, *A Myth of Innocence: Mark and Christian Origins* (Philadelphia: Fortress, 1988), pp. 75–77, 91–93, 215–224.

11. Jeremias, *New Testament Theology*, vol. 1, p. 92.

12. Blackburn, 'Miracles', p. 362. Even R. Bultmann, *Jesus and the Word* (ET New York: Scribner's, 1934), observed, 'undoubtedly [Jesus] healed the sick and cast out demons' (p. 173).

Chapter 9

1. J. Jeremias, *New Testament Theology*, vol. 1 (ET London: SCM, 1971), pp. 178–203.

2. H. Danby, *The Mishnah* (Oxford: Clarendon, 1933), p. 321.

3. Ibid.

4. See A. C. Thiselton, *The First Epistle to the Corinthians*, New International Greek Testament Commentary (Grand Rapids: Eerdmans, 2000), p. 522.

5. According to Josephus, 'From women let no evidence be accepted, because of the levity and temerity of their sex' (*Antiquities of the Jews* 4.219; tr. L. Feldmann, Loeb Classical Library [Cambridge, Mass.: William Heinemann, 1965], p. 581). Cf. Mishnah, *Roš Hašanah* 1.8; see generally the tractates *Sanhedrin* (the Sanhedrin) and *'Eduyyot* (Testimonies).

6. I employ the word 'zealot' broadly; the Zealot faction did not arise until c. 67.

Chapter 10

1. The Aramaic words are transliterated in Greek.

2. R. Bultmann, *New Testament Theology* (ET London: SCM, 1952), vol. 1, pp. 42–53.

3. G. Vermes, *Jesus the Jew* (London: Collins, 1973), pp. 103–128.

Chapter 11

1. The title of ch. 2 in E. Schweizer, *Jesus* (ET London: SCM, 1971). Schweizer, however, argues against Jesus' view of himself as Messiah.
2. Jesus is often addressed as 'Lord' in the Gospels, where 'Lord' meant only a courteous 'Sir'.

Chapter 12

1. G. Vermes, *Jesus the Jew* (London: Collins, 1973), pp. 224–225.
2. E. Schürer, rev. and ed. G. Vermes, F. Millar and M. Goodman, *The Jewish People in the Age of Jesus Christ* (Edinburgh: T. & T. Clark, 1979), vol. 2, p. 456.

Chapter 14

1. P. Barnett, *Paul, Missionary of Jesus* (Grand Rapids: Eerdmans, 2008), pp. 57–70.
2. For Paul's baptism in Damascus, see Acts 9:17; 22:12–13, 16; and for his meeting with Cephas and James, see Gal. 1:18–19.
3. Cf. 1 Cor. 11:23: 'For I received from the Lord *what* I also delivered to you'.
4. The Gospel of Matthew refers to the burial chamber as *taphos* (27:61, 64, 66; 28:1).
5. Hos. 6:2 declares, 'After two days he will revive us; / on the third day he will raise us up, / that we may live before him', but this does not explicitly prophesy the resurrection of the Messiah.
6. See N. T. Wright, 'Resurrection in Q', in D. R. Horrell and C. M. Tuckett, *Christology, Controversy and Community* (Leiden: Brill, 2000), pp. 85–97; *The Resurrection of the Son of God* (London: SPCK, 2003), pp. 429–434.
7. *The Phenomenon of the New Testament* (London: SCM, 1967), p. 3.
8. Ibid., p. 17.
9. N. J. Dawood (Harmondsworth: Penguin, 1956), p. 382.
10. J. D. M. Derrett, *The Anastasis: The Resurrection of Jesus as an Historical Event* (Shipton-on-Stour: Drinkwater, 1982).

11. A view associated with K. Lake, *The Historical Evidence for the Resurrection of Jesus* (New York: Putnam, 1907).

12. F. Collins, *The Language of God* (New York: Free, 2006), pp. 221–223.

13. W. L. Craig, 'Resurrection and the Real Jesus', in P. Copan (ed.), *Will the Real Jesus Stand Up?* (Grand Rapids: Baker, 1998), p. 160.

14. Quoted in J. R. W. Stott, *Basic Christianity* (Leicester: IVP, 1974), p. 47.

Chapter 15

1. Literally, 'We *gospel* you, that what God promised to our fathers he has fulfilled to us their children'.

2. B. Jowett, quoted in F. F. Bruce, *The Acts of the Apostles* (Grand Rapids: Eerdmans, 1990), p. 34.

3. See C. Hemer, *The Book of Acts in the Setting of Hellenistic History*, Wissenschaftliche Untersuchungen zum Neuen Testament 49 (Tübingen: Mohr, 1989), pp. 423–424. The elements that have been recognized are the *proem* text (1 Sam. 13:14) chosen by the preacher as a means of linking the *seder* (Torah reading) (Deut. 4:37–38) and the *haftarah* (reading from the Prophets) (1 Sam. 7:6–16). The preacher delivered the homily by a process called *haruzin*, the 'stringing of beads'. Various authorities on synagogue preaching have discerned these characteristics in Acts 13:16–41.

Chapter 16

1. *Thiasos* (for example) described a group of persons who met to worship a deity.

2. Not all share this view, preferring Rome as the location of these readers.

3. Tr. B. Radice, Loeb Classical Library (Cambridge, Mass.: William Heinemann, 1969), pp. 285–291.

4. Rome and Corinth (Acts 18:2), Ephesus (Acts 18:18; 1 Cor. 16:19), Rome (Rom. 16:3), Ephesus (2 Tim. 4:19).

Chapter 17

1. Tr. L. Feldmann, Loeb Classical Library (Cambridge, Mass.: William Heinemann, 1965), pp. 49–50.
2. Ibid., p. 495.
3. Tr. J. Jackson, Loeb Classical Library (Cambridge, Mass.: William Heinemann, 1956), pp. 283–285.
4. Tr. M. Harris, 'References to Jesus in Early Classical Authors', in D. Wenham (ed.), *Gospel Perspectives 5* (Sheffield: JSOT, 1984), p. 345.

Chapter 18

1. In addition to manuscripts of Matthew, Mark, Luke and John, texts survive of the *Gospel of Thomas* (Papyrus Oxyrhynchus 1), *The Gospel of Peter* (Papyrus Oxyrhynchus 4009), an 'Unknown Gospel' (Papyrus Egerton 2), Valentinus' *Gospel of Truth*. There are also patristic references to the *Gospel of the Ebionites* (Irenaeus, *Against Heresies* 1.26.2; 3.21.1), the *Gospel of the Nazoreans* (Eusebius, *History of the Church* 4.22.8), the *Gospel of the Hebrews* (Clement, *Miscellanies* 2.9.45).
2. *Philadelphians* 7.1 ('the Spirit . . . knoweth not whence it comes or whither it goes') appears to echo John 3:8 (tr. K. Lake, Loeb Classical Library [Cambridge, Mass.: William Heinemann, 1992], p. 245).
3. Revelation was not written until the mid-90s, explaining why it is not quoted in the early past-apostolic writings.
4. *Trallians* 9.4, quoted in J. N. D. Kelly, *Early Christian Creeds* (London: Longmans, 1963), p. 68.
5. *Philippians* 2; Kelly, *Early Christian Creeds*, p. 70.
6. Kelly, *Early Christian Creeds*, p. 72.
7. See R. Bauckham, *Jesus and the Eyewitnesses* (Grand Rapids: Eerdmans, 2006), pp. 417–420.
8. See P. W. Comfort, *The Quest for the Original Texts of the New Testament* (Grand Rapids: Baker, 1992), pp. 31–32.
9. A. Roberts and J. Donaldson (eds.), *The Ante-Nicene Fathers* (Grand Rapids: Eerdmans, 1884), vol. 1, p. 164.
10. E.g. Matt. 1:22 (*First Apology* 33), Mark 2:17 (*Dialogue with Trypho* 8), Luke 1:32 (*First Apology* 33) and John 3:5 (*First Apology* 61).

11. H. I. Bell and T. C. Skeat, *Fragments of an Unknown Gospel and Other Early Christian Papyri* (London: British Museum, 1935).

12. E. C. Colwell, Review of Bell and Skeat, *Unknown Gospel*, in *Journal of Religion* 16.4 (1936), pp. 478–480.

13. See further, C. A. Evans, *Fabricating Jesus* (Downers Grove: IVP, 2007), p. 89.

14. So P. A. Mirecki, 'Peter, Gospel of', in D. N. Freedman (ed.), *Anchor Bible Dictionary*, 6 vols. (New York: Doubleday, 1992), vol. 5, pp. 278–281.

15. See P. M. Head, 'On the Christology of the Gospel of Peter', *Vigiliae christianae* 46.3 (1992), pp. 209–224.

16. Ibid., p. 218.

17. C. M. Tuckett, 'Thomas and the Synoptics', *Novum Testamentum* 30.7 (1988), pp. 132–157; 'Synoptic Traditions in Some Nag Hammadi and Related Texts', *Vigiliae christianae* 36 (1982), pp. 173–190.

18. For a generally negative assessment of the value of the apocryphal Gospels, see J. H. Charlesworth and C. A. Evans, 'Jesus in the Agrapha and Apocryphal Gospels', in B. Chilton and C. A. Evans (eds.), *Studying the Historical Jesus* (Leiden: Brill, 1994), pp. 479–533.

19. A. Roberts and J. Donaldson (eds.), *The Ante-Nicene Fathers* (Grand Rapids: Eerdmans, 1884), vol. 2, p. 416.

20. Ibid. 1.3.6.

21. Irenaeus reports (*Against Heresies* 3.3.4) that when Polycarp met Marcion, he called him 'the first-born of Satan' (Roberts and Donaldson, *Ante-Nicene Fathers*, vol. 2, p. 416).

22. Ibid. , p. 429.

23. Ibid., p. 428.

24. The dating of the emergence of the codex is not known, and remains a subject of debate. T. C. Skeat, 'The Origin of the Christian Codex', in J. K. Elliott (ed.), *Collected Biblical Writings of T. C. Skeat* (Leiden: Brill, 2004), pp. 79–87, conjectures that Christians began using the codex for the Gospels as early as AD 100. See further L. Hurtado, *The Earliest Christian Artifacts* (Grand Rapids: Eerdmans, 2006), pp. 43–89.

25. Roberts and Donaldson, *Ante-Nicene Fathers*, vol. 2, p. 414.

26. Tr. K. Lake, Loeb Classical Library (Cambridge, Mass.: William Heinemann, 1992), p. 397.

SELECT BIBLIOGRAPHY

BARNETT, P., *The Birth of Christianity* (Grand Rapids: Eerdmans, 2005).

———, *Jesus and the Rise of Early Christianity* (Downers Grove: IVP, 1999).

BAUCKHAM, R., *Jesus and the Eyewitnesses* (Grand Rapids: Eerdmans, 2006).

BULTMANN, R., *New Testament Theology* (ET London: SCM, 1952).

CROSSAN, J. D., *The Birth of Christianity: Discovering What Happened in the Years Immediately After the Execution of Jesus* (San Francisco: HarperCollins, 1998).

EVANS, C. A., *Fabricating Jesus* (Downers Grove: IVP, 2007).

EVANS, C. A., and CHILTON, B. (eds.), *Studying the Historical Jesus* (Leiden: Brill, 1994).

HENGEL, M., *The Four Gospels and the One Gospel of Jesus Christ* (ET London: SCM, 2000).

———, *Studies in Early Christology* (Edinburgh: T. & T. Clark, 1995).

HURTADO, L., *The Earliest Christian Artifacts* (Grand Rapids: Eerdmans, 2006).

JEREMIAS, J., *New Testament Theology*, vol. 1 (ET London: SCM, 1971).

MEIER, J. P., *A Marginal Jew: Rethinking the Historical Jesus*, vol. 2 (New York: Doubleday, 1994).

MOULE, C. F. D., *The Phenomenon of the New Testament* (London: SCM, 1967).

VERMES, G., *Jesus the Jew* (Glasgow: Collins, 1973).

WRIGHT, N. T., *The Resurrection of the Son of God* (London: SPCK, 2003).

INDEX OF SCRIPTURE REFERENCES

INDEX OF ANCIENT SOURCES

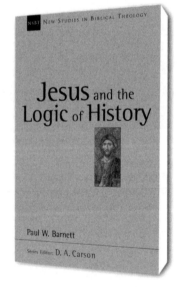

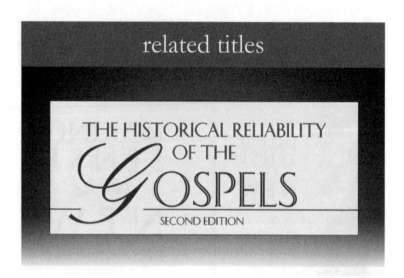
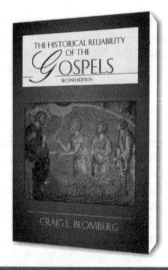

related titles

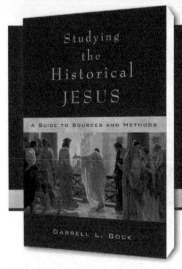

Studying
the
Historical
JESUS

A GUIDE TO SOURCES AND METHODS

Interest in the historical Jesus continues to occupy much of today's discussion of the Bible. The vexing question is how the Jesus presented in the Gospels relates to the Jesus that actually walked this earth.

Studying the Historical Jesus is an introductory guide to how one might go about answering that question by historical inquiry into the material found in the Gospels. Darrell Bock introduces the sources of our knowledge about Jesus, both biblical and extra-biblical. He then surveys the history and culture of the world of Jesus. The final chapters introduce some of the methods used to study the Gospels, including historical, redaction, and narrative criticisms.

Darrell Bock, a well-respected author, provides an informed evangelical alternative to radical projects like the Jesus Seminar. His audience, however, is not limited only to evangelicals. This book, written for college and seminary courses, offers an informed scholarly approach that takes the Gospels seriously as a source of historical information.

ISBN:
978-0-85111-273-2

Available from your local Christian bookshop or via our website at **www.ivpbooks.com**

Dictionary OF
Jesus AND THE
Gospels

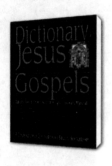

The *Dictionary of Jesus and the Gospels* is unique among reference books on the Bible, the first volume of its kind since James Hastings published his *Dictionary of Christ and the Gospels* in 1909.

In the decades since Hastings, our understanding of Jesus, the evangelists and their world has grown remarkably. New interpretive methods have illumined the text, the ever-changing profile of modern culture has put new questions to the Gospels, and our understanding of the Judaism of Jesus' day has advanced in ways that could not have been predicted.

The *Dictionary of Jesus and the Gospels* bridges the gap between scholars and those pastors, teachers, students and lay people desiring in-depth treatment of select topics in an accessible and summary format.

The *Dictionary of Jesus and the Gospels* presents the fruit of evangelical New Testament scholarship at the end of the twentieth century – committed to the authority of Scripture, utilizing the best of critical methods, and maintaining dialogue with contemporary scholarship and challenges facing the church.

ISBN:
978-0-85110-646-5

Available from your local Christian bookshop or via our website at **www.ivpbooks.com**

www.ivpbooks.com

For more details of books published by IVP, visit our website where you will find all the latest information, including:

Book extracts   Downloads
Author interviews Online bookshop
Reviews   Christian bookshop finder

You can also sign up for our regular email newsletters, which are tailored to your particular interests, and tell others what you think about this book by posting a review.

We publish a wide range of books on various subjects including:

Christian living   Small-group resources
Key reference works   Topical issues
Bible commentary series Theological studies